Should the U.S. Close Its Borders?

Other Books in the At Issue Series:

Affirmative Action

Animal Experimentation

Can Busy Teens Succeed Academically?

Can Celebrities Change the World?

Club Drugs

How Safe Is America's Infrastructure?

Nuclear Weapons

The Olympics

Polygamy

Teen Smoking

Teen Suicide

The U.S. Policy on Cuba

What Is the Future of the Music Industry?

What Is the Impact of E-Waste?

What Is the Impact of Tourism?

What Role Should the U.S. Play in the Middle East?

At Issue

Should the U.S. Close Its Borders?

David Haugen, Susan Musser, and Kacy Lovelace, Book Editors

GREENHAVEN PRESS
A part of Gale, Cengage Learning

Detroit • New York • San Francisco • New Haven, Conn • Waterville, Maine • London

Christine Nasso, *Publisher*
Elizabeth Des Chenes, *Managing Editor*

For more information, contact:
Greenhaven Press
27500 Drake Rd.
Farmington Hills, MI 48331-3535
Or you can visit our Internet site at gale.cengage.com

Articles in Greenhaven Press anthologies are often edited for length to meet page requirements. In addition, original titles of these works are changed to clearly present the main thesis and to explicitly indicate the author's opinion. Every effort is made to ensure that Greenhaven Press accurately reflects the original intent of the authors. Every effort has been made to trace the owners of copyrighted material.

LIBRARY OF CONGRESS CATALOGING-IN-PUBLICATION DATA

Should the U.S. close its borders? / David Haugen, Susan Musser, and Kacy Lovelace, book editors.
p. cm. -- (At issue)
Includes bibliographical references and index.
ISBN 978-0-7377-4689-1 (hardcover) -- ISBN 978-0-7377-4690-7 (pbk.)
1. Border security--United States--Juvenile literature. 2. United States--Emigration and immigration--Juvenile literature. 3. National security--Law and legislation--United States--Juvenile literature. I. Haugen, David M., 1969- II. Musser, Susan. III. Lovelace, Kacy.
JV6483.S55 2010
325.73--dc22

2009044270

Printed in the United States of America
1 2 3 4 5 6 7 14 13 12 11 10

Contents

Introduction

Securing the U.S. borders is a formidable task. The United States maintains over three hundred ports of entry—stations set up to receive visitors, immigrants, returning U.S. citizens, and legally transported goods coming into the country. These ports of entry are staffed with administrators and clerks who are trained to handle any problems that may arise. Any or all of these ports of entry could be closed, if necessary, but they are not the only points of access into the country. Goods or people can also sneak into the United States along more than seven thousand miles of land boundaries that span deserts, mountains, plains, lakes, and rivers. In addition, the United States is bounded by thousands of miles of coastline, some of it extending to the Arctic Circle. The manpower, fences, and other barriers necessary to completely shut off or monitor all these boundaries are not, in a practical sense, feasible.

The U.S. Customs and Border Protection agency (CBP) is the primary force that oversees the nation's borders. Its ancestor, the U.S. Immigration Service Border Patrol, was founded in 1924 to stop the entry of illegal immigrants and curtail smuggling. Since September 11, 2001, however, the mission of the CBP (now part of the Department of Homeland Security) has been expanded. CBP agents are now also concerned with preventing terrorists and weapons of mass destruction from entering the country. The roughly 20,000 field members of this group are given the job of monitoring the northern and southern land borders, while U.S. Customs officials and the Coast Guard watch air and sea lanes.

The U.S. border with Canada is the longest common border in the world at just short of four thousand miles. This border stretches from the Pacific to the Atlantic oceans and includes the shorelines of four of the Great Lakes. Another land line separates Canada from the state of Alaska, adding 1,538 miles to the northern border. For decades, this border was mostly undefended, as relations between the United States and Canada have mostly been friendly. Then, in 1999, Ahmed Ressam, an Algerian nicknamed the Millennium Bomber, was stopped at the U.S.–Canada border. Driving a car loaded with explosives, he planned to blow up parts of Los Angeles International Airport. Canadian law enforcement tracked him, and he was eventually stopped by U.S. border patrol agents in Washington. A trial and conviction put Ressam in jail, but his capture also alerted the United States that its northern border was threatened. As Jean-Louis Bruguiere, a French terrorism judge, warned the conservative Internet news service *Insight on the News*, "If your Customs people hadn't been lucky, there would have been a major attack in America, with many dead."

Since Ressam's crossing and the September 11, 2001, terrorist actions, security has been increased so that the U.S.–Canada border is a less-porous point of entry. Unmanned predator B drones—originally developed for military missions—were first deployed on the northern border in 2009. These remote-controlled aircraft conduct surveillance along the waterways between New York and Ontario. They join a host of other high-tech gadgets used to stop illegal crossings. Video cameras mounted on eighty-foot towers, radiation sensors, and infrared technologies now assist agents in securing the hitherto undefended boundary. Furthermore, in years past, Canadian and U.S. citizens could cross over the border for dinner or a day trip without presenting identification, but now passports or other forms of identification are required. But even with increased security, only one percent of illegal entries into the United States are caught at the northern border.

Another one and a half percent of illegal entries are stopped along the U.S. coast. This vast coastline extends a total of 12,383 miles and is patrolled regularly by ship and aircraft to keep illegal immigrants, terrorists, drugs, weapons, and other contraband from landing on U.S. shores. Much of the U.S. Customs seagoing focus is on Florida and the area around the U.S. territory of Puerto Rico—key points of entry for drug traffickers. The U.S. Navy and Coast Guard assist in securing the U.S. coastline against the drug trade as well as against the entry of illegal aliens.

To the south, the U.S. border with Mexico extends 1,933 miles and crosses four U.S. states: California, Arizona, New Mexico, and Texas. Significantly, ninety-one percent of the people who enter the United States illegally come from Mexico, and another seven percent are from Central American countries. The U.S.–Mexico border, where ninety-seven percent of illegal entries into the country occur, is therefore the primary focus of border control policy.

The southern border is difficult to monitor. While CBP agents cover many well-worn paths of entry, illegal entrants are determined and often blaze new routes through harsh desert terrain. The CBP, therefore, relies on motion sensors, cameras, radar, and dogs to track the movements of aliens and smugglers. Government agents also use deterrents to keep illegal travelers from making attempts. Something as simple as installing bright lights has helped slow the rate of illegal crossings in places, but the most talked-about deterrents are the various barriers and walls used to seal off common points of entry.

In 2006, Congress voted to install 670 miles of security fences at points along the southern border with Mexico. To date, this project has not been completed, and its cost has risen to about a million dollars per mile. Its effects have been mixed and the subject of controversy. In some areas—Yuma, Arizona, for example—the number of illegal immigrants attempting to cross the border has dropped dramatically. Speaking of the barrier, one Yuma border agent told the *Christian Science Monitor*, "A lot of people have the misconception that it is a waste of time and money, but the numbers of apprehensions show that it works." In other regions, however, tunnels and blowtorches have thwarted the fence. Some believe its presence has only pushed those that are determined to get into the United States into more desolate and dangerous border areas.

By 2009, more than 580 miles of fence had been installed, some of it erected to stop pedestrians and some to stop vehicles. Different types of fencing appear in different areas. The fences designed to stop cars and trucks are often made of uneven pillars (bollards) spaced a yard or so apart. Some of these vehicle fences have wire mesh as well to block pedestrian access. Other sections of the U.S.–Mexico border are guarded by tall barriers made of pipes or chain link, sometimes topped with barbed wire and usually anchored in concrete.

It is a matter of debate whether the structural barriers are responsible for the drop in illegal entries in recent years. Indeed, the number of people arrested for trying to enter the United States illegally has declined from 1,676,000 in 2000 to 724,000 in 2008—the lowest number of apprehensions in twenty-five years. The heightened border security and increased number of agents may have had a deterrent effect, but factors such as lower employment opportunities in the United States and U.S. companies moving manufacturing operations to Mexico may also play a role. Dawn McLaren, a research economist, predicts, "If the economy improves and the Border Patrol continues its efforts, we should see more arrests at the border."

At Issue: Should the United States Close Its Borders? explores the controversy over the methods of border control and the soundness of these policies. Advocates of a strictly monitored border believe that in an era of terrorism and economic instability, the United States needs to protect its borders. In their view, health care costs, job security, and national defense rely on the nation stemming the tide of illegal immigrants.

Champions of a more open immigration policy, however, maintain that strong borders are as diplomatically unfriendly as they are easy to outwit. They contend that although more should be done to keep out dangerous threats, the majority of illegal aliens are simply seeking opportunities to work in a land that holds a promise for a better life. In the twin ages of globalization and terrorism, border policy will have much to do with how the United States fares as a nation of freedom, opportunity, and security in coming times.

1

Terrorism and Border Control: An Overview

Edward Alden

Edward Alden is a senior fellow at the Council on Foreign Relations, a public-policy think tank in Washington, D.C., and New York City, and the former Washington, D.C., bureau chief for the Financial Times [London]. *He is also the author of the 2008 book* The Closing of the American Border: Terrorism, Immigration, and Security since 9/11.

Although it has been more than eight years since the September 11, 2001, terrorist attacks on the United States, the general reaction to even a minor threat within the U.S. borders is often one of panic and severely heightened security. To contend with the possibility of further terrorist incidents and to identify and diffuse potential threats, the Department of Homeland Security was established in 2003. This governmental body has enacted several national security defense measures, including the tightening of visa regulations and the implementation of US-Visit, a system of fingerprinting travelers to the United States. However, the most daunting task the Department of Homeland Security faces is securing the borders the United States shares with Canada and Mexico. These vast stretches have never been completely safeguarded, though various plans and projects have been tried in the name of keeping criminals, illegal immigrants, and terrorists out of the country.

Edward Alden, "The Quest for the Perfectly Secure Border," *Canada Watch*, February 25, 2009. Reproduced by permission.

Andrew Speaker had at least this in common with a terrorist: he was determined not to be caught. Speaker, a U.S. citizen, had been warned by American health authorities in May of 2007 to stay at home in Atlanta after he contracted a highly-infectious, drug-resistant strain of tuberculosis (TB). But he had plans to be married in Europe, so he ignored the warning and flew to Paris. Two weeks later, after U.S. officials had tracked him down in Rome, he promised to get treatment there and refrain from traveling. Yet the next day he broke his word and boarded a flight from Prague to Montreal, where he rented a car and drove across the U.S. border at Champlain, New York. When the news broke, it became Exhibit A for those who think that porous borders remain the biggest threat to U.S. security. Congress immediately convened hearings to vent its outrage at the Department of Homeland Security. If a known TB carrier could be waved into the country across the northern border, they argued, how much harder could it be for one of [al Qaeda terrorist leader Osama] bin Laden's operatives?

The reaction to Speaker's sojourn was a warning about what is still to come as the mentality of "homeland security" becomes ever more firmly entrenched in Washington, despite the years that have passed since the 9/11 [2001 terrorist] attacks. The administration of Barack Obama may change the nuances and nudge the priorities, but it is a worldview that is shared by Democrats and Republicans alike. And it will make life still more complicated and difficult for America's neighbours on its northern and southern borders.

Creating a New Agency to Combat Vulnerabilities

Since its establishment in 2003 at the urging of congressional Democrats, the Department of Homeland Security (DHS) has conceived its mission as one of plugging vulnerabilities. For the United States, this was a radically new concept. In its modern history, America had always defended itself far from it borders, either fighting wars abroad or deterring the handful of adversaries capable of striking U.S. territory by threatening massive retaliation. While 9/11 did not abolish that paradigm, it certainly altered it. Since suicide terrorists could not be deterred, the reasoning went, they must be kept outside the United States.

That launched the quest for the perfectly secure border, and it has brought a gradually escalating effort to deploy people, technologies, and old-fashioned barriers to keep the "bad guys" out of the United States. It began with the most obvious threats revealed by the 9/11 attacks, but has since fanned out to ever more ambitious efforts to protect against ever smaller threats—not just terrorism but drug runners, illegal migrants, and careless travelers with communicable diseases. It is an approach that has its own expansive logic: once you plug one gap in the border defences, the next one on the list looms that much larger.

The U.S. list began, quite reasonably, with the [September 11] hijackers themselves. All nineteen [al Qaeda operatives] had come from Middle Eastern countries on validly issued visas, so the first step was to tighten visa procedures, especially from countries known to have an al-Qaeda presence. All had flown to the U.S., so Washington forced airlines to turn over their passenger lists for all future incoming flights. At least two, and possibly more, should have been on U.S. terrorist watch lists, so Washington broke down internal barriers to information sharing and added hundreds of thousands of names. Those measures—more careful visa scrutiny, advanced information on incoming passengers, and a robust, if not terribly discriminating, terrorist watch list—probably went 90 per cent of the way to keeping out al Qaeda operatives. But that's where it started to get complicated. As terrorism experts point out, al Qaeda is an adaptable adversary, so once the obvious routes to the United States were blocked, they could be expected to look for others.

The biggest concern was Europe. Most Europeans can travel to the United States without first getting a visa. As the London and Madrid train bombings showed, Europe has a handful of radicalized Muslims prepared to attack civilians. So as the price for maintaining the visa waiver program, the United States forced European nations into a series of concessions. The Europeans agreed to hand over detailed advanced information on all passengers flying into the United States despite the problems this caused under Europe's more stringent privacy rules; they would alert Washington when any blank passports were stolen, which had been an endemic problem in countries like Belgium; and they would share information on their own lists of terrorist suspects.

Due to the sheer volume of crossings, the land borders pose special, and possibly insurmountable, problems for an approach to homeland security premised on plugging vulnerabilities.

Fingerprinting U.S. Visitors

Then in early 2004, the United States launched the fingerprinting scheme euphemistically known as US-VISIT [United States Visitor and Immigrant Status Indicator Technology program]. It was originally conceived in the 1990s as a way to stop visa overstayers, who are thought to make up as much as 40 percent of illegal immigrants living in America. But after 9/11 it was repackaged and sold on terrorism grounds. For most travelers to the United States, that now means getting fingerprinted twice—once when you get the visa, and again when you arrive in the United States. For most Europeans, Japanese and citizens of other visa waiver countries, it just happens once.

Washington announced recently that the scheme would be expanded to include permanent residents or green card holders living in the country. Not surprisingly given its origins, it has done nothing to identify terrorists, but DHS points out that more than 4,000 criminals and immigration violators have been stopped. Not a threat on par with terrorism, to be sure, but who could object to keeping criminals and unauthorized migrants out of the country?

As each of these vulnerabilities was checked off the U.S. to-do list after 9/11, the next item rose in priority. That has brought us to where we are today, with much of the focus on the northern and southern land borders. Due to the sheer volume of crossings, the land borders pose special, and possibly insurmountable, problems for an approach to homeland security premised on plugging vulnerabilities. Mexicans are already facing stricter identification requirements at the southern border, which has produced further delays in the already gridlocked ports of entry. Canadians, and Americans crossing the northern border, are set to face the same as of June 2009 unless Congress pushes the deadline back again, which is unlikely.

The problem with the perfect border is that we live in an imperfect world—a world of ill-defined threats and fallible people trying to respond to them.

Mexicans and Canadians, in most cases, are not routinely fingerprinted when they come to the United States. Yet under laws already passed by Congress, they are supposed to be, and DHS is experimenting with ways to make that happen without stalling cross-border traffic entirely. And the entry fingerprint is only step one. Congress has also mandated that every visitor should "check out" of the country as well. For stopping terrorists, this has almost no value, but it would be helpful for immigration control. DHS has recently proposed that airlines collect the fingerprints from departing airport passengers, which has the airline industry up in arms. No one has any good ideas about how to do this at the land borders, but it is inching up on the to-do list of vulnerabilities.

Imperfect Barriers and Failed Strategies

Finally, if the legal ports of entry can be secured, the long undefended borders will then become the biggest threat. Ever more of the Mexican border has been fortified in the name of keeping out drugs and illegal migrants. About 500 miles of steel fence are already in place. President Obama's new homeland security secretary Janet Napolitano—who knows that border well as a former Arizona governor—is a critic of the fence, but has been enthusiastic about a "virtual fence" composed of surveillance cameras, unmanned aerial drones, and heat-sensing technologies. So far the pilot projects have failed dismally, but once the kinks are worked out the same schemes are likely to be rolled out along the Canadian border.

The question arises: could any of this have kept Typhoid Andy from returning home to Atlanta? Possibly, but not necessarily. U.S. border inspectors had been warned to watch for him, but the inspector at Champlain ignored the warning and let him in anyway. And it turns out he wasn't all that contagious after all and does not appear to have infected anyone.

The problem with the perfect border is that we live in an imperfect world—a world of ill-defined threats and fallible people trying to respond to them. The United States needs some way to distinguish urgent and serious threats from minor ones and to calculate the costs—to the economy, to relations with neighbours and allies, and to its tarnished image as an open and welcoming society—of trying to counter those threats. In other words, the United States needs a strategy, not just a series of reactions. That is the real border challenge for the Obama administration, but not one, sadly, that it is likely to embrace.

2

U.S. Borders Must Be the First Line of Defense

Stewart Baker

Stewart Baker was the first assistant secretary for policy at the Department of Homeland Security—a position he held from July 2005 to January 2009, during the administration of George W. Bush. He previously served as general counsel to the National Security Agency under President George H.W. Bush. Baker is currently affiliated with Steptoe and Johnson LLP in Washington, D.C.

U.S. security from terrorist threats relies on identifying and tracking the movements of known and suspected terrorists. The automated targeting system used by the Department of Homeland Security has helped turn away dangerous individuals from U.S. borders. Using flight information and passport data, the system can uncover links that would prompt border agents and travel security officers to investigate suspicious foreign visitors. Such individuals need to be screened and turned away at the border because once they are in the United States they are more difficult to track.

I'm going to talk today about how DHS [Department of Homeland Security] screens for terrorism risks at our borders, and in particular how we use travel reservation data to do that. I'm going to talk first about how our automated targeting system works. Then I'll address some of the criticisms of the program, first the claim that the program was somehow

Stewart Baker, "Protecting Our Borders," *Vital Speeches of the Day*, vol. 73, February 1, 2007, pp. 58–60. Reproduced by permission of the author.

sneaked into operation without notice and then the claim that the program is bad for civil liberties.

A Terrorist Turned Back at the Gate

Before I do that, though, I'd like to begin with an event far from our borders. In Iraq, in February 2005, at about 8:30 in the morning, several hundred police recruits were lining up outside a clinic in Hilla.

You know what happened next.

A young Jordanian man drove into the crowd and detonated a massive car bomb. 132 people died, and about as many were wounded. It was the most deadly suicide bombing Iraq had seen.

The driver's name was Ra'ed al-Banna. We know that because the authorities found the steering wheel of his car, and his forearm was still handcuffed to it.

But I'm not here to talk about what al-Banna did in 2005. I'm here to talk about what he didn't do in June of 2003.

That's when al-Banna showed up at O'Hare Airport in Chicago and asked to be admitted to the United States. He had a legitimate passport in his own name. He had a valid visa. But he didn't get in.

Why not? Because data in the DHS computer system flagged him as someone who ought to get a bit more scrutiny than the usual passenger. So he was interviewed, using some of the data in the system. In the end, the officer who did the interview decided that al-Banna's answers weren't consistent. So the officer denied him admission, and sent him back to Jordan.

No one knows why al-Banna wanted to enter the U.S. in 2003—or what he would have done if he'd gotten in. And personally, I'm glad we didn't get the chance to find out.

Next time we may not be so lucky. That's because the computer system that first flagged al-Banna for scrutiny is suddenly being attacked as an invasion of travelers' privacy

There are calls to abolish it or restrict how DHS uses it. Those calls are wrong, and I'd like to show why by explaining how the system works.

The Screening Process

Hundreds of millions of people enter the U.S. each year—including 87 million by air. Our job is to move them quickly and smoothly through immigration and customs. That's a big customer-service challenge. In fact, if we take more than a minute or two with each traveler, the lines will back up out to the tarmac.

But our first mission is not to move those travelers through. Our first mission is to keep terrorists out of the country. So, did you ever wonder how we can identify potential terrorists just by glancing at their passports and asking a couple of questions?

The answer is that we can't. That quick interview is where we screen travelers. Most people go right through. But a few of them are sent to "secondary" inspection, where officers can spend more time asking more questions.

We might have been able to uncover the [September 11, 2001] plot if we'd had better computer systems and better access to travel data.

How do our officers decide who needs a closer look? Some of it is based on training and experience and intuition. Some of it is data in the passport. But their main tool is the computer system that helped stop Ra'ed al-Banna—the Automated Targeting System, or ATS. ATS means faster service for most travelers. It also means that we're smarter and more consistent about who gets a closer look.

Here's how it works. When people buy plane tickets, they give the airline some information—names, passport numbers, frequent-flyer numbers, credit cards, and so on. DHS collects

this information from the airlines and uses ATS to do screening for dangerous people. ATS runs the travelers' names against lists of known or suspected terrorists. It can also do a quick link analysis, looking for travelers who gave the airline a phone number that's also used by a known terrorist.

Lessons from September 11

ATS's capacity to find hidden links of this kind is one of its most powerful features. This is a lesson we learned from September 11 [2001]. After-the-fact reviews of the hijackers' travel reservations showed that we might have been able to uncover the plot if we'd had better computer systems and better access to travel data.

Start with two men who helped fly American Airlines flight 77 into the Pentagon: Nawaq Alhamzi and Khalid Al-Midhar. Their names appeared on a U.S. watch list, because they had been spotted at a terrorist meeting in Malaysia. So they would have been flagged when they bought their tickets.

If we had kept tugging on that thread, we would have found three other hijackers who used the same addresses as the first two—including Mohamed Atta, the plot's ringleader. We also would have discovered another hijacker who used the same frequent-flyer number. That's six of the 19.

And we're not done. Five other hijackers used the same phone number as Mohamed Atta. That's eleven of 19. We could have found a twelfth hijacker in an INS [Immigration and Naturalization Services] watch list for expired visas, and the remainder could have been flagged by matching other basic information.

We didn't connect those dots before 9/11, but we should have. We learned that lesson, and now ATS allows us to look for these links.

I wish DHS could take full credit for ATS, but the need to screen airline passengers isn't exactly an original thought. Contrary to the claim that this program was launched in the dead of the night, it has a long and proud pedigree. This is the second point I promised to discuss.

Targeting Terrorist Travel

Faced with the evidence that we had been unable to find the 9/11 hijackers, here's what the 9/11 Commission [in its report released on July 22, 2004] had to say:

> Targeting travel is at least as powerful a weapon against terrorists as targeting their money. The United States should combine terrorist travel intelligence, operations, and law enforcement in a strategy to intercept terrorists, find terrorist travel facilitators, and constrain terrorist mobility.

The 9/11 Commission did more than just embrace passenger screening in the abstract. It specifically endorsed ATS, and called for its expansion:

> The small terrorist travel intelligence collection and analysis program currently in place has produced disproportionately useful results. It should be expanded. . . . Information systems able to . . . detect potential terrorist indicators should be used at consulates, at primary border inspection lines, in immigration services offices, and in intelligence and enforcement units.

It's hard to find a more specific recommendation in the Commission's report. In fact, if we hadn't already built ATS, we could expect legislation in the first 100 hours of the next [2007] Congress, ordering us to build it.

But Congress doesn't need to do that, because Congress has already authorized the use of travel reservation data to screen for security risks.

Congressional Support

Just after the 9/11 attacks, Congress passed the Aviation and Transportation Security Act, which requires airlines to share reservation information about all U.S.-bound passengers with

DHS. Now I suppose that our critics could argue that Congress just wanted us to gather the data and not to actually, you know, use it. We could avoid a charge of "data mining" if we just boxed the data up and put it in storage. But no serious person thinks that's what Congress had in mind. Congress expected us to do exactly what we have been doing.

Finally, if any doubt remains about Congress's support for ATS, just look at DHS's budget. In this city, money talks. And Congress has appropriated money specifically for the ATS passenger-screening program—for instance, $37 million in 2005 and $28 million in 2006.

Let me stop here for a moment and emphasize that Congress's demand for better screening at the border has not to date been a partisan issue. The 9/11 Commission, of course, was entirely bipartisan—and unanimous in calling for better screening. The 2001 Aviation and Transportation Security Act that mandated collection of this data had overwhelming Democratic support. There were no recorded dissents when it passed the Senate and it got 200 Democratic votes in the House.

No Threat to Privacy

In short, both parties in several Congresses have affirmed that we need to flag terrorists who may be coming to the U.S. and that we need to make passenger information available to DHS inspectors. It would be hard to imagine a program that stands on firmer legal ground than ATS.

ATS [the Automated Targeting System] does not pose a threat to privacy.

Who could be against it? Well, predictably, privacy groups have denounced it as an unnecessary government surveillance program. That's the third point I promised to discuss—whether this program is bad for civil liberties.

I'll start with a song from the 1980s called "Somebody's Watching Me."

When I come home at night,

I bolt the door real tight.

People call me on the phone, I'm trying to avoid.

Well, can the people on TV see me or am I just paranoid?

We've all heard that sometimes "even paranoids have enemies." That's true, but the corollary is that much of the time, they are just paranoid. Certainly that's true in the case of ATS.

The fact is that ATS does not pose a threat to privacy. First, ATS is not exactly a dossier of our most intimate secrets. It contains travel reservation data—flight numbers and destinations and traveling companions. Travelers have already chosen to give it to Lufthansa to make their flight a little more convenient. How are they harmed if DHS uses it to make sure they actually arrive at their destination?

We also work hard to protect that information from abuse. To get access to ATS, employees have to pass a background check and have an active security clearance. Some of the most sensitive bits of data can only be seen by supervisors. And users of ATS are closely audited. All system queries are logged, and can be traced back to the employee who did the analysis. We have zero tolerance for misuse of the system. All misconduct is punished; an employee who breaks the rules faces penalties that range from suspension to termination.

Finally, let's look at the other side of the equation. If the most extreme privacy advocates got their way and shut the program down, how exactly do they expect us to protect ourselves from terrorists?

They don't like programs that put everyone through the same screening, like our airport security programs. They say it's silly to make grandmothers and infants go through all these searches. But they think selecting some travelers for greater scrutiny on the basis of limited information is even worse. That leads to profiling and searches based on stereotypes rather than real data. Everyone agrees that race and religion shouldn't be the basis for inspecting travelers. But when we gather more individualized information and look for links to terrorist credit card numbers or addresses, the critics say we're building a national database that threatens privacy. What's left? It seems as though the only thing these groups would let DHS do to prevent an attack is to pray it won't happen. As long as we don't pray in public.

ATS isn't just a useful tool against terrorists. It has also helped break up international crime syndicates.

Using ATS to screen for passengers who should get a second look is better for civil liberties—and for security—than any of those alternatives. It's also more effective.

A Viable System That Keeps Terrorists out

Ra'ed al-Banna is not the only person that ATS has helped keep out of the country. It happens every day. Just a few months ago [in 2006], at Minneapolis-St. Paul, ATS flagged a high-risk traveler for additional scrutiny before he arrived. Once we got him into secondary inspection, we found that he had a manual on how to make Improvised Explosive Devices, or "IEDs"—the kind of bombs terrorists use to kill and maim so many of our troops in Iraq and Afghanistan. Our officers also found video clips of IEDs being used to kill soldiers and destroy vehicles, as well as a video on martyrdom. This was a dangerous man, and we are all safer because ATS flagged him for scrutiny.

ATS isn't just a useful tool against terrorists. It has also helped break up international crime syndicates. In March 2004, a woman returned to Newark International Airport from the Dominican Republic, accompanied by her children. CBP [Customs and Border Protection] officers examined ATS data and noticed that the woman hadn't taken the kids with her on the outbound flight. They did some more digging and discovered that the woman had made numerous such trips before. Each time she left without the children; each time she returned with them.

ATS also allowed the officers to link this woman to other travelers. And it turned out that some of them had the same travel patterns—they would leave the U.S. alone, and come back with children. It was an international child-smuggling ring, and ATS helped us take it down.

In conclusion, let me just remind everyone that the border is our last, best chance to identify and turn away terrorists. Once they're in the country, they're much harder to find and much harder to stop. We need the best possible information on the hundreds of millions of people who cross the border every year. ATS helps us marshal that information. It helps us protect Americans from terrorism, and the more Americans understand it the more confident I am that they will support it—with enthusiasm.

3

U.S. Borders Should Be the Last Line of Defense

Margaret D. Stock

Margaret D. Stock is a member of the American Immigration Lawyers Association as well as a lieutenant colonel in the U.S. Army Reserves. Stock works as an associate professor in the department of social sciences at the U.S. Military Academy at West Point in New York, where she teaches international relations and provides expertise on various topics relating to immigration, law, and security.

Current programs to stop terrorists at America's borders are not effective. Strict immigration laws and burdensome policies that impede legitimate foreign visitors discredit the nation and do little to prevent terrorist traffic. Instead, U.S. policy should aim at greater intelligence gathering to identify and track known terrorists before they reach America's borders. In addition, the government needs to reform immigration laws to understand why and how immigrants cross borders and to keep track of undocumented individuals in the country.

Our current immigration system is an obstacle to enhancing our security because it is dysfunctional and unenforceable. We currently allocate massive resources in a futile attempt to enforce a system that simply does not work. Continuing to enforce our currently dysfunctional system will

Margaret D. Stock, "The Need for Comprehensive Immigration Reform: Strengthening Our National Security," Remarks made before the Joint Senate Committee on the Judiciary Subcommittee on Immigration, Border Security, and Citizenship, and the Subcommittee on Terrorism, Technology, and Homeland Security, May 17, 2005, pp. 6–11.

only lead to more dysfunction and a waste of resources. On the other hand, comprehensively reforming our laws will shrink the haystack of people so that we separate those who are here to be with their families or work from those who aim to do us harm. Our enforcement efforts would be far more effective if our laws made sense. In considering reforms to those laws, what are the questions we need to ask and answer?

A Fortress America Is Counterproductive

What security measures are most effective in preventing attacks? In the hours following the deadly terrorist attacks of September 11, 2001, the United States government took the extraordinary step of sealing U.S. borders to traffic and trade by grounding all aircraft flying into or out of the country and imposing a lock-down on the networks of transportation and commerce that are the lifeblood of our economy and society. Given the uncertainty over what might happen next, these emergency procedures were a necessary and appropriate short-term response to the attacks. In the long run, however, a siege mentality and the construction of a fortress America are ineffective and unrealistic responses to the dangers we face.

If we are to succeed in reducing our vulnerability to further terrorist attacks, we must focus our attention and resources on the gaps in intelligence gathering and information sharing that allowed nineteen terrorists to enter the United States. National security is most effectively enhanced by improving the mechanisms for identifying actual terrorists, not by implementing harsher immigration laws or blindly treating all foreigners as potential terrorists. Policies and practices that fail to properly distinguish between terrorists and legitimate foreign travelers take us down the wrong path as ineffective security tools that do more harm than good. Comprehensively reforming our immigration laws is an essential tool to help us distinguish between those who mean to do us harm and those who are here to fill our labor market needs and reunite with close family members.

As Asa Hutchinson [the first under secretary for border and transportation security at the Department of Homeland Security] rightly stated when he appeared before this [Senate] committee last year [in 2004], "Illegal entry across our borders makes more difficult the urgent task of securing the homeland. Our homeland will be more secure when we can better account for those who enter our country, instead of the current situation in which millions of people are unknown."

If we are going to take seriously our responsibility to defend the homeland, we must make hard choices and do what is needed to know who is here, who is entering, and why. In pursuit of answers to these questions, DHS has developed several programs, some in conjunction with other departments. Some of these initiatives include:

- The National Targeting Center [NTC], which provides around the clock tactical targeting and analytical research support for anti-terrorism efforts. The NTC staff consists of CBP [Customs and Border Protection] officers and field analysis specialists who are experts in identifying high-risks targets from raw intelligence, trade, travel, and law enforcement data;
- The Human Smuggling and Trafficking Center, a joint DHS, DOS [Department of State], and DOJ [Department of Justice] venture that analyzes and disseminates information to enforcement, intelligence and other entities that take action against threats of human smuggling, trafficking and against criminal support for terrorist travel; and
- Threat Analysis Section (TAS), an ICE [Immigration and Customs Enforcement]-run program that identifies and addresses potential vulnerabilities to the United

> States. The TAS establishes associations between the individuals or groups linked to potential national security threats, develops profiles based upon relevant investigative and intelligence reporting, and produces actionable leads for field office.

To enhance our security we must make our physical borders the last line of defense against terrorism, not the first.

I hope that one of the main questions the Senate asks as a result of this hearing is how comprehensive immigration reform would help these anti-terrorism programs be more effective? The answer is clear. By bringing the people that are here out of the shadows, and creating an orderly mechanism for identifying and documenting the low-risk individuals who travel to this country to work, and by curbing policies such as separating families that entice otherwise low-risk individuals to cross the border illegally, a comprehensive immigration reform plan would help these initiatives better focus on those who have come here to do us harm. Quite simply, only an immigration reform program that deals with the current problem in its entirety would have such a positive effect. A program that fails to identify the reasons for illegal-crossings or one that inadequately deals with the undocumented population would not help these initiatives protect our citizens.

The recent [2005] enactment of the REAL ID Act [which sets federal standards for state-issued driver's licenses] makes these efforts more important than ever. REAL ID forces states to stop putting data provided by illegal immigrants into the largest law enforcement database in the country—the driver's license database. When only American citizens and legal aliens are in this database, border security and interior enforcement will be harder than ever to accomplish. Comprehensive immigration reform is thus also necessary to counteract the security vulnerability the REAL ID Act has created.

Current Border Programs May Be of Limited Use

What is the role of our "borders" in enhancing security? What and where are our borders? When people refer to our "borders," they usually mean the geographic boundaries that separate the United States from Canada and Mexico. Yet to enhance our security we must make our physical borders the last line of defense against terrorism, not the first. We must pursue initiatives including multilateral strategies with Canada and Mexico and increase the use of pre-clearance and pre-inspection programs that provide U.S. officials the opportunity to check passengers for admission before those passengers board a flight to the United States (while including safeguards to allow asylum protection for those who truly deserve it).

Our government has been touting the United States Visitor and Immigrant Status Indicator Technology program (US-VISIT) [implemented in 2004] as a tool that will help to make us safer by identifying terrorists. While US-VISIT can help to identify people, its utility as a security tool is unclear. This new automated entry/exit system is being implemented at our nation's ports of entry and is designed to collect and share information on foreign nationals traveling to the United States (including travel details and biometric identifiers), confirm identity, measure security risks, and assess the legitimacy of travel in an effort to determine who is welcome and who is not. The program is also intended to help speed traffic flow. The overall plan for the implementation of US-VISIT calls for the collection of personal data, photos, and fingerprints at U.S. consular offices abroad and at our ports of entry, as well as broad database and information sharing. The system also is intended to track changes in foreign nationals' immigration status and make updates and adjustments accordingly. Ultimately, the Department of Homeland Security (DHS) plans to make available information captured through US-VISIT at all ports of entry and throughout the entire immigration enforcement system.

Will US-VISIT help to enhance our security? While the jury is still out, serious questions need to be addressed as to US-VISIT's achievable mission. A June 1998 Senate Judiciary Committee Report makes the following apt comment:

> The Committee is keenly aware that implementing an automated entry/exit control system *has absolutely nothing to do* with countering drug trafficking, and halting the entry of terrorists into the United States, or with any other illegal activity near the borders. An automated entry/exit control system will at best provide information only on those who have overstayed their visas. Even if a vast database of millions of visa overstayers could be developed, this database will in no way provide information as to which individuals might be engaging in other unlawful activity. It will accordingly provide *no assistance in identifying terrorists, drug traffickers, or other criminals.* (emphasis added)

With regard to tracking visa overstayers, the report further states:

> Even if a list of names and passport numbers of visa overstayers would be available, there would be no information as to where the individuals could be located. Even if there was information at the time of entry as to where an alien was expecting to go in the United States, it cannot be expected that 6 or more months later the alien would be at the same location. Particularly, if an alien were intending to overstay, it is likely that the alien would have provided only a temporary or false location as to where the alien was intending to go.

Notwithstanding these concerns, to enhance our security and allow the flow of people and goods to support our economy, US-VISIT must be adequately funded. The U.S. government needs to appropriate billions of dollars to purchase real estate, upgrade facilities, develop an infrastructure and technological capabilities, and hire inspectors to manage the program. This cost includes neither the millions of dollars needed to fully address current staffing shortages of inspectors at ports of entry nor the money now needed to supply all ports with basic technology such as document readers. With a preliminary estimated price tag of billions of dollars, recent appropriations have been grossly insufficient to fund the program's expansion. Without sufficient funding to support a fully operational program, delays could result in the entry and exits at our nation's ports, particularly land ports. Such delays would undermine the entire effort to maintain an efficient border, and efficiency is a vital component of increased security.

In addition, as the number of enrollees into US-VISIT increases, it is incumbent upon the Department of Homeland Security to ensure that information input into the database is accurate and reliable. This includes integrating into US-VISIT the databases from the three immigration bureaus. Unless these databases are integrated with US-VISIT, visitors who have applied for visa extensions might be detained for overstaying their visas, when in reality, they had maintained proper visa status. Having complete and correct information will make the difference between having a workable secure system or a discredited inefficient one.

As we think about our security needs, we must remember that we need a strong economy to pay for our national security.

While US-VISIT is still in its infancy, database studies and reports should be completed on the feasibility of every aspect of the program. The Administration and Congress should use that information to develop a comprehensive plan that takes into account adequate funding levels, resources, and obtainable deadlines.

The Need for a Virtual Border Approach

How do we balance the flow of people and goods with securing our borders? The United States has over 300 ports of entry through which authorized travelers and commercial goods enter the country. In 2001, over 510 million people (63% of whom were foreign nationals) and over $1.35 trillion in imports entered the U.S. through these ports. If the inspection of each of these entrants took even a little longer than it currently does, the flow of goods and people (particularly at land ports) would come to a grinding halt. The Department of Homeland Security thus has the challenge of streamlining current border procedures and evaluating future initiatives so that the border crossing processes are both more secure and efficient. Otherwise, security measures that do not take into account travel and trade could cripple our nation's economic viability. As we think about our security needs, we must remember that we need a strong economy to pay for our national security.

Deficiencies in U.S. intelligence collection and information sharing, not immigration laws, prevented the [September 11, 2001] terrorists' plans from being discovered.

Our economic prosperity depends on the free movement of people and goods. We must be careful not to create an environment conducive to terrorists and criminals at our ports-of-entry as we seek to secure our borders in a way that does not trump cross-border facilitation. We need to adopt a "virtual border" approach that recognizes the importance of the continued flow of people and goods, and underscores that effective border management needs to take place away from our physical borders. I would only add that comprehensively reforming our immigration laws is the other component that is necessary for our borders to work and work well because such reform helps identify the people who present themselves at our ports-of-entry, thereby making legality the norm.

Using Available Tools and Enacting Further Reforms

What is the role of immigration in the post-September 11 world? Because all nineteen of the September 11th terrorists were foreigners, some observers have been quick to blame our vulnerability to terrorist attacks on lax immigration laws. While such a response was predictable, it was misguided and has inevitably resulted in overreaction. Calls to impose a "moratorium" on immigration, halt the issuance of student visas, close the borders with Canada and Mexico, eliminate the Diversity Lottery visa program [which grants permanent resident visas to countries with low rates of immigration to the United States], draft harsher immigration laws, and similar types of proposals reflect a serious misunderstanding of the relationship between immigration policy and national security.

Although the attacks of September 11th revealed serious management and resource deficiencies in the bureaucracies that administer our borders, U.S. immigration laws in and of themselves did not increase our vulnerability to attack. In fact, U.S. immigration laws already are among the toughest in the world and have long provided the federal government with broad powers to prevent anti-American terrorists from entering or residing in the United States. A careful analysis of the September 11th attacks reveals that deficiencies in U.S. intelligence collection and information sharing, not immigration laws, prevented the terrorists' plans from being discovered.

The Use of Technology. Technology is not a magic bullet. The best way to identify terrorists is an approach that capitalizes on human intelligence, using technology only to enhance our ability to use human intelligence. Our greatest successes in preventing terrorist attacks have come not from technology identifying terrorists, but from human intelligence we have gathered about terrorists. Over-reliance on technological solutions to the detriment of creating a strong human intelligence program is a recipe for disaster.

Proper Use of Databases. In creating and relying on ever-larger computer databases, we must be aware of the limitations of such databases and the potential security vulnerabilities that we are creating. In some cases, we are planning to rely heavily on the use of databases for purposes for which they were not intended. For example, the use of the NCIC [National Crime Information Center] database to track civil immigration violations presents difficulties in that immigration status is a moving target. A person can be legal one day, illegal the next; or legal one day, illegal the next, and legal again the following day. Using the NCIC database to track such violations is likely to make that database much less useful to law enforcement officials because there will be more inaccurate data in the system than there is already. The REAL ID Act has ruled out the possibility of using state DMV [Department of Motor Vehicles] databases as a source of information about the illegal or undocumented migrant population in the United States. Thus, REAL ID will make it harder to enforce immigration laws, not easier. Comprehensive immigration reform that allows illegal immigrants to come out of the shadows and be identified will enhance our security and improve government data on who is present in the United States.

Is it important to move ahead on comprehensive immigration reform to secure our borders? Yes, absolutely. Our nation has no choice but to move ahead on comprehensive immigration reform if we are to secure our borders, enhance our security, and create a safe, legal, orderly and controlled immigration system.

4

Keeping the Borders Open Harms U.S. Workers

Steven A. Camarota

Steven A. Camarota is director of research for the Center for Immigration Studies (CIS). Since he started working for the CIS in 1996, Camarota has authored and co-authored more than 100 reports, testimonies, and opinion editorials (op-eds) pertaining to his areas of expertise, which are economics and demographics.

Today immigrants are arriving in the United States faster than they have at any other time in history. Unfortunately, the majority of immigrants who come to the United States are poorly educated, and they take jobs away from undereducated U.S. citizens. These less-educated legal immigrants can be a burden to taxpayers because they strain social services. The United States should focus on reforming immigration laws to keep more low-skilled immigrants out of the country.

The United States needs fewer immigrants, not more. Lower levels of immigration, both legal and illegal make sense for my country because the growing number of undereducated people crossing our borders have hurt less educated native-born workers. The U.S. needs to focus on reducing overall immigration levels. This means a drop in the number of immigrants from Latin America, which accounts for half of the new arrivals, many of them at the lower end of the educational spectrum.

The number of immigrants—legal and illegal—living in the U.S. is growing at an unprecedented rate. U.S. Census Bu-

Steven A. Camarota, "Immigration Is Hurting the U.S. Worker," *Americas Quarterly*, Spring 2007. Reproduced by permission.

reau data indicate that 1.6 million legal and illegal immigrants settle in the country each year. In 2006, the immigrant, or foreign-born population, reached about 38 million in the United States. Roughly 12 million of these were illegal aliens. Legal and illegal immigrants now account for one out of every eight persons living in the United States. As recently as 1970 the proportion was one in twenty residents. The U.S. has never confronted an immigrant population that has grown this much, this fast.

Hurting the Poor

Low-paid American workers have borne the heaviest impact of immigration. This is largely because of the educational profile of the bulk of today's immigrants. Nine percent of adult native-born Americans (ages 18 to 64) were high school dropouts in 2006, while 34 percent of recent adult immigrants had not completed high school. (The rate was 60 percent for illegal immigrants.)

The disproportionate flow of undereducated immigrants to the U.S. has . . . depressed wages for native-born workers on the lower rungs of the economic ladder.

Common sense, economic theory, and a fair reading of the research on this question indicate that allowing in so many immigrants (legal and illegal) with relatively little education reduces the wages and job prospects for Americans with little education. These are the Americans who are already the poorest workers. Between 2000 and 2005, the number of jobless natives (age 18 to 64) with no education beyond a high school degree increased by over two million, to 23 million, according to the Current Population Survey. During the same period, the number of less-educated immigrants (legal and illegal) holding a job grew 1.5 million.

Of greater concern, the percentage of employed native-born without a high school degree fell from 53 to 48 percent in the last five years [2002–2007]. African Americans have particularly been affected. A September 2006 National Bureau of Economic Research paper found that immigration accounted for about a third of the decline in the employment rate of the least-educated African American men over the last few decades.

The disproportionate flow of undereducated immigrants to the U.S. has also depressed wages for native-born workers on the lower rungs of the economic ladder. In the last two-and-a-half decades, average hourly wages for male workers with less than a high school education declined more than 20 percent relative to inflation. For those with only a high school degree they are down almost 10 percent.

Typically, pro-immigration voices argue that immigration is essential because there are not enough Americans to fill all the low wage jobs. But if this were so, then the wages and employment rates of such workers should be rising as employers try desperately to retain and attract workers. Yet quantitative evidence for such a phenomenon doesn't exist. The only evidence of a labor shortage comes from the employers.

The biggest problem for taxpayers is not illegal aliens . . . the biggest problem is less-educated legal immigrants.

In addition to harming the poorest and least educated American workers, our immigration system has created a large burden for taxpayers. The best predictor of poverty and welfare dependence in modern America is education level. Given the low educational levels of most recent immigrants, we would expect them to be a greater drain on public coffers than the immigrants who came before them. Indeed this is the case. In 1997 the National Academy of Sciences (NAS) estimated that immigrant households consumed $20 billion more in public services than they paid in taxes each year. Adjusted for inflation, with the current size of the immigrant population today, this figure would be over $40 billion.

The Burden to Taxpayers

Immigrants from Latin America place an especially heavy burden on American taxpayers. For example, 57 percent of households headed by Dominican immigrants in 2004 used at least one major welfare program; 43 percent of Mexicans took advantage of at least one welfare program; and about a third of the households headed by immigrants from Central America, Cuba and Columbia use the welfare system. In contrast only 18 percent of native households receive welfare assistance.

The biggest problem for taxpayers is not illegal aliens—though they are a drain. The biggest problem is less-educated legal immigrants, who represent the majority of the immigrants from Mexico and Central America. My own research indicates that the net costs (taxes paid minus services used) to the federal government alone would roughly triple if illegal aliens were legalized and began to use services and pay taxes like legal immigrants with the same level of education.

Even if one conceded that allowing in less-educated immigrants is bad for less-educated Americans, are there any economic benefits from immigration? The best research on the subject shows that if there is a benefit it is tiny or "miniscule," in the words of the nation's top immigration economist, George Borjas of Harvard University. The NAS study found that by reducing the wages of the least-educated Americans (about 10 percent of the population), immigration generated an economic benefit for the rest of society equal to just two-tenths of one percent of their income.

One common argument for immigration is that American society is aging. We are told that we need young workers. But demographers have found that immigration actually has only a small impact on this problem. The 2000 Census showed that

66.2 percent of the population was of working age (15 to 64). If all post-1980 immigrants (legal and illegal) and their U.S.-born children are not counted, the working-age share would still have been 65.9 percent in 2000.

The current system, which allows people into the country if they have a family member here, is simply not sustainable. The goal of reform should be an immigration system that allows in fewer low-skilled immigrants. Actually enforcing current immigration laws would be a good first step.

5

Keeping the Borders Open Does Not Harm U.S. Workers

Martin Oppenheimer

Martin Oppenheimer is an associate professor of sociology and labor studies at Rutgers University, The State University of New Jersey. He is the author of several books about the civil rights movement and radical sociology, including The State in Modern Society *and* The Hate Handbook: Oppressors, Victims, and Fighters.

Though some analysts assert that immigrant workers are displacing undereducated native-born U.S. workers—especially African American workers—many studies have shown the opposite. The impact of deindustrialization and the outsourcing of costly labor—rather than the influx of immigrants—have had a more damaging effect on labor in the United States. It may appear that immigrants shut native-born workers out of jobs (specifically low-paying, low-skill positions), but the claim is debatable. Niche industries exist for all ethnic or racial groups, and this pattern of "preferential" employment has not changed over the years, despite the rise in immigration. In addition, certain industries keep wages so low that only desperate immigrants would take the jobs offered, proving there are some forms of work native-born workers will not do because of living standards, the inability to relocate, or other barriers.

Do immigrants have a deleterious effect on U.S.-born, especially African-American workers, as has been charged by any number of writers, from Christopher Jencks to the Center for Immigration Studies' George Borjas to Stephen Steinberg (writing in [*New Politics*], summer 2005 and winter 2006)? Does immigration add to their costs especially in unemployment, underemployment, and wages? Do immigrants survive, never mind rise, on the backs of the native-born proletariat, especially African-American workers? Whatever else immigrants are charged with, it is these questions, and their answers, that are crucial to understanding and overcoming divisions within the U.S. working class (the primary one being white versus all workers of all other colors, the second the division between Latinos and Blacks). What strategy to develop to overcome these divisions is crucial to the future of progressive politics in this country.

Massive migration from all parts of the globe began after the immigration reforms of 1965. The result was that immigrants were "thrust into competition with blacks for job opportunities," according to Steinberg, author of the highly regarded *The Ethnic Myth*. He asks, are African-American workers becoming superfluous because immigrants (including the undocumented) have arrived in such large numbers so as to undercut Black progress? He assumes that the jobs are there: "Although it is often argued that blacks arrived [in urban job markets] at a time when the industries that had provided opportunities to earlier immigrants were in decline, the fact is that millions of new immigrants were rapidly absorbed into both the residual blue-collar sector and the expanding service industries." He states that if immigration had remained at the low level of 1965, then "tight labor markets would have provided incentives for employers to lower their racist barriers, to hire and train black workers, and if necessary, to improve wages and conditions to make even these marginal jobs attractive to native workers."

What has happened, Steinberg says, is that the presence of immigrant labor has kept wages down, sidelined African-American labor (via discrimination), and in some cases has even led to the exodus of African-Americans from some communities. Although Steinberg comes at the issue from what he sees as a left perspective, the gist of his argument is little different from that of Jencks, Borjas, or any of the writers who want to stop, or at least slow-down, immigration. He dismisses studies concluding that immigration has only small negative effects on the economic situation of African-Americans. This, he says, defies common sense given the horrendous unemployment statistics for Black men in so many urban areas.

Deindustrialization, Not Immigration, Hurts African-American Workers

In the follow-up issue of *New Politics*, Michael Hirsch, a sociologist and labor journalist, concentrates on the structural factors that historically pushed and pulled Black workers into Northern and Western cities, resulting in significant economic advances (the push factor of collapsing agricultural prices and continuing racism in the South, and the pull factor of wartime jobs in both World Wars). Deindustrialization is the major factor that has destroyed these advances and has pauperized large sectors of the industrial heartland and cities dependent on manufacturing generally. This is where the African-American population came to be concentrated after World War II. "The tragedy of deindustrialization," he says, "is that the closing of the mills liquidated this generation of well-paid black breadwinners and the shop-floor leadership that was emerging." Immigration was not a factor in that, nor, for instance, in the containerization process in the shipping industry, or in the computerization of auto plants, among other examples. Hirsch summarizes: If the U.S. had limited immigration instead of liberalizing it post-1965, then "outsourcing of U.S. products and services would have happened that much sooner." This point is made by a number of researchers. For example, Nelson Lim, a researcher at RAND [the RAND Corporation, a nonprofit research organization], writing in Roger Waldinger's edited *Strangers at the Gates* [2001], puts it succinctly: "In the era of (NAFTA [North American Free Trade Agreement]), any decline in the supply of low-skilled immigrants will simply push employers to move their businesses abroad." The point is not so much that if labor costs become too high labor will be exported. "Too high" is after all simply a cost factor determined by competition and profit rates. It is that if labor costs are lower elsewhere, work will be moved there so long as it can be.

And if it cannot be moved? In the absence of immigrants, would African-American (and white) workers be mowing lawns, cleaning hotel rooms, and nailing up sheetrock (jobs that are not exportable) at union-level wages? Following Steinberg's argument, would white employers hire African-American workers in a more or less nondiscriminatory way because they were needed, as they once were in heavy industry, if immigrants were not available?

The Components of the Immigration Issue

To get at some answers to this and the broader question of whether or not immigrants are undermining U.S.-born labor, it is useful to break the issue down into three discrete parts: (1) are immigrants hired in preference to U.S.-born, especially African-American workers? (2) do immigrants displace U.S.-born, especially African-American workers? (3) does immigrant competition lower the wages of U.S.-born workers? The short answer to each of these questions is: Yes and No, Sometimes, and Maybe. Whatever else, the answer is not an unequivocal Yes, despite what anti-immigrationists from the Minutemen [a civilian organization that patrols the U.S.–Mexico border] and [television commentator] Lou Dobbs on the "populist" right to some unions, and even some respected researchers, say. This brief essay can do no more than summarize. But first it should be made clear that any social science research that relates to policy is political: there is no "objective" or "neutral" methodology. Immigration research is no exception.

Network hiring, all experts agree, is crucial in creating employment niches for many (not only immigrant) ethnic/racial groups.

Are immigrants hired in preference to U.S.-born, especially African-American workers? There is a consensus about one aspect of this allegation at least: employers, especially of younger, lower skilled, less educated workers, often hire immigrants (generally Latinos) over African-Americans. As Steven Camarota, Director of Research at the Center for Immigration Studies [C.I.S.] told the U.S. House Committee on the Judiciary on Oct. 30, 2003, "There is certainly a lot of anecdotal evidence and some systematic evidence that immigrants are seen as better workers by some employers, especially in comparison to native-born African Americans." Roger Waldinger and Michael I. Lichter, in their 2003 book *How the Other Half Works*, devote an entire chapter to addressing "Whom Employers Want," and conclude that employers have a "hierarchy of ethnic preferences" in which African-Americans are at the bottom. As Andrew Sum, also associated with the C.I.S., told an American Youth Policy Forum in March 2005, there is "a perceived reputation of many immigrants as hard-working and loyal," with the implication that African-American youth are not, that they have "attitudes" that make them less reliable, more troublesome, employees.

As for the realities underlying these preferences, any number of observers, including scholars, have pointed to the employment consequences of "ghetto-related behavior," as

African-American sociologist William Julius Wilson, a former President of the American Sociological Association put it, which is by no means limited to African-American youth. There are a lot of reasons for dysfunctional (to job-seeking) behavior among some lower stratum working class youth, but understanding them doesn't change employers' discrimination. We don't actually know the extent of these behaviors, but we do know that many employers buy into these stereotypes. In support of the discrimination thesis Andrew Sum cites data showing that among low-income male high school students 23 percent of whites, 12 percent of Hispanics, but only 7% of African-Americans are employed.

Stephen Steinberg, in his *New Politics* essays, challenges the accuracy of employer claims, and says that even if this stereotype has a basis in fact, employers are obligated to hire on the basis of individual merit and not on the reputation of the group. For him it's plain old-fashioned prejudiced, racist-based discrimination. More to the point, he says employers use "network hiring" of immigrants to keep African-Americans out. Network hiring, all experts agree, is crucial in creating employment niches for many (not only immigrant) ethnic/racial groups. Once an employer hires a worker who proves reliable, the employer will ask that worker to recruit another, who will likely be of the same ethnicity. In that it excludes other ethnicities, network hiring constitutes a form of institutional racism, true enough, but hiring that relies on referrals from present employees is universal. Why is this "naked bigotry" (Steinberg's expression) when African-Americans are excluded (consciously or not), but not when they do the "excluding" as they develop niches, as in several of the Los Angeles industries described by Waldinger and Lichter? Employment niches, sociologist Frank Wilson noted several years ago, involve a "substantial share of the workforce of urban minority workers": 37 percent of African-Americans, 36 percent of Hispanics, and 27 percent of Asians. Of course the reasons for the development of these niches vary. Frequently they are the result of exclusion from other occupations. And minorities create businesses that cater to specialized minority markets. Regardless of the reason an ethnic quasi-monopoly or niche develops in an occupation, or in a business, other groups tend to stay away. Short of legally mandating hiring halls for all employment, a political impossibility, network or nepotistic hiring will continue in the private sector, and will, naturally, cause resentment among those excluded.

There appears to be no decline in native, including African-American, entrepreneurship in major immigrant-receiving areas.

Competitive Structures in Immigrant-Receiving Areas

Aside from discrimination, some econometricians argue that the sheer number of immigrants entering particular occupations will create a competitive structure leading to more unemployment and lower wages for African-Americans. Using a worst-case scenario, George Borjas estimates that the 1980–2000 influx of immigrants might in theory have reduced the employment rate of African-American men by 5 percent at the national level, and in addition increased the incarceration rate of black high school dropouts by 1.7% (the incarceration rate, he says, is correlated to unemployment). But as Borjas admits, "much of the decline in employment and increase in incarceration . . . would have taken place even if the immigrant influx had been far smaller." Presumably this would have been due to deindustrialization rather than to immigration. In any case, immigrants are increasingly dispersed away from urban areas in recent years, so they are not competing as much with African-Americans for jobs in large urban centers, formerly the gateways for all immigration.

As for immigrant enterprises taking business away from native-owned, particularly Black-owned companies, while there are a lot of stories, there is little hard evidence. A 1997 study by Robert Fairlie and Bruce Meyer of U.C. [University of California] Santa Cruz and Northwestern University [Evanston, Illinois] found that immigration had no effect on Black self-employment. Steven Camarota, in a 2000 C.I.S. report arguing that the positive effects of immigrant entrepreneurship have been overrated, indirectly confirms this. There appears to be no decline in native, including African-American, entrepreneurship in major immigrant-receiving areas.

Do immigrants displace U.S.-born workers? The answer is mired in methodological controversies, pitting one set of researchers, those generally associated with the Center for Immigration Studies who, with only a few qualifications, say "Yes" against a range of others whose conclusions are more mixed, more nuanced.

There is some agreement on the dynamic underlying the increasing employment of immigrants at the lower end of the economy. Immanuel Ness, writing in the left *Dollars and Sense* (Sept.–Oct. 2006) tells us that "industrial restructuring and capital mobility have eroded traditional industries . . . in ways that have led many companies to create millions of low-wage jobs and to seek vulnerable workers to fill them." Employers try to maximize profit by making labor cheaper. They increasingly do this through outsourcing or subcontracting, hiring part-timers, and in some industries paying workers under the table. The influx of immigrants provides many of those workers since U.S.-born workers without a high school degree, who are the most vulnerable in our labor force, are now just 12 percent of all U.S.-born workers. So as businesses restructure, if insufficient numbers of U.S.-born workers are available (or those who are available are deemed undesirable) immigrants are hired. Some of them are no doubt among the estimated 6.3 million "illegal" workers in the U.S. economy (4.3 percent of the civilian labor force).

Andrew Sum and colleagues at the C.I.S. pretty much agree: "(S)ome employers have begun to reorganize work in ways that systematically exclude certain native-born workers, especially those under 35, from employment and that create work that does not meet the basic labor standards that have been developed over the years." But their conclusion is not, as you would expect, to advocate enforcement of labor standards. Rather, they assert that "If the jobs held by new immigrant males aged 16 to 34 were made available to jobless native-born males, then the job deficit among the native born [allegedly 1.7 million in 2005] would be completely eliminated." (The number of new immigrant males in that age group is estimated at 1.85 million.) The assumption of the C.I.S. econometricians apparently is that you simply plug 1.7 million non-immigrants into those 1.7 million jobs, just like that. Wouldn't it be nice if the labor market operated that efficiently. In real life, workers do not have perfect information about where jobs are, and even if they did many would not, and often could not (due to age) move, willy-nilly, away from family, friends, churches, neighborhoods, to chase jobs in faraway places unless they were indeed desperate, as desperate, say, as many . . . immigrants.

It would be nice if living wages were available throughout the economy, but in highly competitive, non-unionized, labor-intensive small business sectors, wages are low . . . and desperate immigrants are often willing to take them.

Are Immigrant Laborers Necessary?

So one question is: does the U.S. economy need immigrant workers because there aren't enough U.S.-born workers available? Anti-immigrationists say no, there are enough available, and if there were no immigrants the U.S.-born (including African-American) unemployed would be hired, and discrimination against African-Americans would have to decline. Some pro-immigrationists argue that immigrants are needed because there are jobs "Americans won't do," to which the anti-immigrationists reply, "there are no jobs Americans won't do, you just have to provide decent wages and working conditions."

Are there jobs at the less-skilled end of the occupational spectrum that "Americans won't do," that is, for which they are not available? Maybe there are. The term "available" can mean many things. Many African-American youth are not "available" for field agricultural work because the pay is too low (the average wage of a field agricultural worker is $9.50 an hour), it might require a move to another state, and perhaps there is an onus on doing work associated with slavery. And surely there are other jobs where the pay and working conditions are below what a U.S.-born worker would consider even minimally survivable. It would be nice if living wages were available throughout the economy, but in highly competitive, non-unionized, labor-intensive small business sectors, wages are low and will remain as low as the law allows (or lower, off the books) and desperate immigrants are often willing to take them.

Rob Paral, at the Immigration Policy Center, a branch of the pro-immigrant American Immigration Law Foundation, argues that immigrants are hired to supplement, rather than displace, the U.S.-born, at least in some job categories. "Thirteen occupational categories collectively would have been short more than 500,000 workers during the 1990s without recently arrived immigrant employees, even if all unemployed natives with recent experience in those categories had been re-employed." These jobs include everything from farm workers to cooks, painters, janitors, maids, and construction workers. Moreover, Paral demonstrates that not all immigrants get wages significantly below those of similarly educated and skilled U.S.-born workers, although many do. The unionized workers at Swift Co. in Greeley, Colorado, who were raided by Immigration and Customs Enforcement in December 2006, were earning $12.75 an hour, not a magnificent wage but more than twice the Federal minimum wage. As immigrants become naturalized and get older, their wages approach or exceed U.S.-born workers' wages. This trend will likely continue as more immigrants join unions.

One set of researchers looks at specific geographical areas (usually states), or at specific industries. For example, the Pew Hispanic Center, in an August 2006 report by Rakesh Kochbar, tells us that there are wide variations in the relationship between the growth of immigrant populations and the employment outcomes of U.S.-born workers. About 25 percent of them live in states where growth of immigration is correlated to favorable outcomes for native workers. About 15 percent live in states where the outcome is negative. The rest live in states where immigrant growth was below average, but employment for the U.S.-born wasn't good either. "The size of the foreign-born workforce is also unrelated to the employment prospects for native workers." Even more interesting, the Pew report says, "the relative youth and low levels of education among foreign workers appear to have no bearing on the employment outcomes of native workers of similar schooling and age." Still, it is clear that a much lower percentage of young African-Americans are employed than other groups. That doesn't prove that Hispanics are displacing African-Americans, but questions remain.

Segregating into Ethnic Niche Industries

Another approach, associated with the work of Roger Waldinger and Michael Lichter, focuses on specific industries, in this case in Los Angeles. They examine six low-wage industries and find that the concentration of Latino immigrants and African-Americans differs. Each industry contains disproportionally large components of one or the other. They argue that overall even when immigrants create a "niche" in, say, the apparel industry, and over time displace some U.S.-born workers, the industry's strength in turn creates more jobs for the U.S.-born, at higher wages. "A city experiencing an influx of immigrants may well find itself with more buying power," thus benefiting the job situation for natives. So maybe native workers in positive growth areas would not have been better off without immigration.

Since many immigrants' jobs are in sectors created by immigration itself—the many niche businesses that cater to immigrants—this might well create some kind of multiplier effect, generating more jobs also for the U.S.-born.

What accounts for the skewed distribution of workers of color in Los Angeles (or any) industries? How do ethnic niches develop? In summary, Waldinger and Lichter tell us, "Immigration is a network-driven process, and the prominent role played by ethnic networks in the labor market makes for ethnic separation." Different industries rely more on network recruitment than others. African-Americans are disadvantaged in this process in L.A. at least because of their smaller numbers relative to Latinos, and because of discrimination. In a period of twenty years (1970–1990), "African-American concentrations in those industries in which immigrants were already overrepresented in 1970 simply disappeared." On the other hand, African-American concentration increased where immigrants were underrepresented in 1970. Meanwhile, African-American educational levels had increased. Thus African-Americans, according to Waldinger and Lichter, were "pulled" rather than "pushed" out of their employment concentrations, moving more into higher-skill sectors where bureaucratic rather than network hiring is the pattern, mainly, that is, in the public sector.

Nevertheless, in this changing environment "the less-skilled members of the [African-American] group who cannot pass the employers' tests may be left out in the cold," especially since they must look for work where immigrants have come, over the years, to predominate. Even when overall employment for African-American workers is stable, "immigration may harm the most vulnerable African-Americans and yet yield no net negative effects on Los Angeles African-Americans as a whole."

Little or No Effect on Native-Born Job Loss

Borjas and others associated with the C.I.S. dispute this approach. As Jencks puts it, "we have to treat the United States as one big labor market, figure out how immigrants change the national distribution of skills, and estimate the effect of these changes on different groups' earnings." Also, they argue, if some U.S.-born workers facing immigrant competition decide to move out, those remaining will correspondingly face a tighter labor market and will not be displaced, creating an artificial impression that things aren't so bad in a particular locality. And, since many immigrants' jobs are in sectors created by immigration itself—the many niche businesses that cater to immigrants—this might well create some kind of multiplier effect, generating more jobs also for the U.S.-born.

In general, apart from the C.I.S. group, researchers going back to the mid-1980s have given us mixed messages. They have told us either that the foreign-born share of the population has no significant effect on U.S.-born employment, or if it does, it is very slight, or that the impact on jobs differs from place to place and industry to industry. We cannot dismiss the idea that a large influx or "labor supply shock" as Borjas & Co. call it, of immigrants, especially at the low-skill end, might have a negative effect on some U.S.-born workers' employment rates, and in some cities and industries, especially among African-Americans. But we also should not accept the unqualified generalization that "immigrants take American workers' jobs away" because this is not only misleading, but politically dangerous.

6

The United States Should Adopt Open Immigration

Anthony Gregory

Anthony Gregory is a research analyst for the Independent Institute, a libertarian public-policy research organization in Oakland, California. Gregory is the editor-in-chief of the Web site for Campaign for Liberty, Texas Congressional Representative Ron Paul's organization, as well as a policy advisor for the Future of Freedom Foundation, a free-market libertarian group.

The United States is a free country whose immigration policy should reflect this fact. Immigration controls are socialist in nature and have led to the expansion of bureaucracy, taxation, and the police state. While critics are correct to claim that current immigration policies burden the welfare system, the solution to the problem is to dispense with the welfare system, not bar immigrants from the country. Immigrants have contributed to the wealth and culture of the United States, and the government should adopt open immigration policies so that this trend may continue to enrich the nation.

Immigration is one of the most difficult and divisive issues for freedom lovers. Many principled libertarians and champions of a free society believe in government restrictions on immigration, either for their own sake or as an interim measure so long as the United States has welfare programs that are presumed to attract immigrants, who then become net recipients of government revenue at the cost of taxpayers.

Anthony Gregory, "In Defense of Open Immigration," *Freedom Daily*, October 1, 2004. Reproduced by permission.

Most arguments against immigration, coming from partisans of freedom, boil down one way or another to the notion that free immigration fosters socialism and moves American society away from the libertarian ideal. It is argued that immigrants use welfare programs and encourage their expansion; or that immigrants modify American culture generally for the worse, bringing from their native countries alien and socialistic ideas; or that free immigration itself constitutes a de facto trespass against the private-property rights of Americans; or some combination of the above arguments is advanced.

Immigration as a Welfare Issue

Some pro-immigration libertarians have attempted to show that illegal immigrants actually receive less in welfare than they pay in taxes or even less than what native-born Americans receive, on average. This argument, as useful as it may be, circumvents the fundamental issues of immigration policy. (I, for one, think that if open immigration overloads the welfare system, causing it to collapse, so much the better.)

In exploring immigration as a welfare issue, let us consider that it is not only opponents of social welfare who oppose open borders because of a perceived relationship between immigration and the welfare issue. European countries with socialist economies oftentimes have extremely strict immigration policies, and citizens of those countries oftentimes see that open immigration threatens their welfare state, which they strive to maintain.

American advocates of social welfare policies also see the incompatibility between their pet programs and a free flow of immigrants. In a recent interview with [former Republican presidential candidate] Pat Buchanan, [four-time independent presidential candidate] Ralph Nader implied such an incompatibility, as well as a conception that the government should centrally plan the economy, when he said, "I don't believe in giving visas to software people from the Third World when we have got all kinds of unemployed software people here." He went on to say,

> This is the reason the *Wall Street Journal* is for an open-borders policy: they want a cheap-wage policy. . . . [Illegal immigrants] should be given all the fair-labor standards and all the rights and benefits of American workers, and if this country doesn't like that, maybe they will do something about the immigration laws.

Nader is willing to bet that an expansion of labor regulations and economic socialism would lead to tighter immigration controls, which he appears to advocate.

No libertarians advocate government welfare, and any welfare problem is ultimately not one of immigration.

Conservatives have at times attempted to restrict the ability of immigrants to receive welfare benefits, such as with the notable 1994 Californian voter initiative, Proposition 187. This is surely a better method to reduce any problems immigration might have regarding the welfare state, when compared to giving the government more power and money to keep out immigrants who only seek work and freedom. It is more politically viable and more realistic and reduces the activity of the state, rather than increasing dependence on it. (Ideally, of course, immigrants would be exempt not only from welfare but from taxes as well. Even more ideally, these exemptions would also apply to citizens.)

All in all, any alleged relationship between free immigration and a growing welfare state is irrelevant to the underlying issue, as pointed out by Hans-Hermann Hoppe, a scholar at the Ludwig von Mises Institute and an opponent of open borders. As Hoppe explains,

> [The effect of immigration on welfare] is not an argument against immigration but against the welfare state. To be

> sure, the welfare state should be destroyed, root and branch. However, in any case the problems of immigration and welfare are analytically distinct problems, and they must be treated accordingly.

No libertarians advocate government welfare, and any welfare problem is ultimately not one of immigration. Though Hoppe is against open borders, he urges us to separate the issues conceptually.

The Cultural Impact of Immigration

Some libertarians, including this writer, often argue that immigration is a blessing to the culture of America, which has always been a nation with a large immigrant population. The expanded variety in foods, music, art, and traditions is one of the things that makes America the great country it is.

The cultural impact of immigration is really secondary to what kind of immigration policy is fit for a free country.

Other libertarians argue that immigrants bring with them foreign customs, practices, and ideas, which, on balance, compromise the tradition of American liberty embraced by native-born Americans, whose Anglo-European heritage provides them with an affinity for the rule of law and constitutional liberty or who simply have assimilated and come to embrace freedom over socialism.

There are weaknesses with this argument, seeing that many immigrants come especially because they seek freedom, not the socialism or despotism characteristic of the countries from which they come. To the extent that they come for the socialism that already exists in America, it testifies as much against the socialist tendencies of Americans, who enact such policies, as it does against the foreigners who seek them.

However, like the welfare issue, the cultural impact of immigration is really secondary to what kind of immigration policy is fit for a free country. Many libertarian policies will tolerate culturally and even morally questionable trends, but we who cherish freedom believe that such vices will pale in importance when compared with the moral virtues and practical benefits of maximized freedom, as well as the moral and cultural greatness that such freedom, on balance, nurtures.

Immigration Controls Are Fraught with Problems

So the real question is whether open immigration or restricted immigration is the more appropriate policy for a free country. One argument against open immigration, given by some libertarians, is that in an ideal world almost all land would be private, but in the meantime illegal immigrants who use public space are essentially trespassing on what should be the privately owned land of native-born Americans.

It is indeed true that we should maximize how much land is owned privately. If nearly all land were private, landlords, employers, merchants, and others would determine who could enter their property. Every property owner would have his own "immigration" policy.

In the meantime, what is the most libertarian immigration policy? The fact is, landlords, employers, and merchants currently allow immigrants on their land all the time, and in many cases would be more open to immigrants if they did not fear legal repercussions. The only question that remains is what to do about public property, including much of the land along the national borders. Whereas in a free society property owners along the border would be free to allow foreigners to enter their property, opponents of open immigration believe that the government must, in the interim, forbid people from allowing immigrants onto their own land.

The philosophical case for prohibiting immigrants on public land—and by corollary, effectively keeping them out of the country and off the private land of willingly accommodating owners—as an extension of private property rights is highly problematic. Why would such a rationale not be fitting to limit, by law, the number of children a family can have? If a middle-class family has 10 children, certainly it takes up an amount of space disproportional to its income and what it pays in taxes.

Just like all other federal government programs, immigration controls are a form of socialism.

Every day we see the willingness of Americans to accommodate immigrants. The market supports them. They work, purchase goods and services, and pay for housing. Their use of public resources and land, if anything, is a problem with the status of so much property as public—just as their potential abuse of welfare is a problem with welfare itself. Continuing to shut out immigrants, or becoming even more restrictive with the borders, further reinforces the notion that so much public land should be protected by government, and takes us a step away from our ultimate goal of eventually privatizing it. Once most land is privatized, most immigrants would be able to find work and housing in the marketplace, and in the meantime the government cannot mimic the proper supply and demand for labor in lieu of market mechanisms.

Furthermore, the use of the federal government to control borders contributes directly to socialism far more than the immigrants themselves.

Just like all other federal government programs, immigration controls are a form of socialism. They involve bloated budgets, bureaucracy, central planning, taxation, abusive police powers, intrusions in the marketplace, and widespread corruption.

Immigration controls are expensive, and they clearly don't work that well. More than a million foreigners enter America illegally every year. A serious attempt to keep them out would require even higher taxes, a more militarized border patrol, and vast invasions of the privacy of employers and other Americans. It would potentially require a national ID card, as well as an army of border police and federal agents to round up and repatriate illegals. It would depend on central planning, which, as all free-market economists should know, simply doesn't work. The border guards have already been implicated in a number of scandals, and the idea that the government can maintain efficiency and honesty in its border police, when the federal government does a poor job of preventing corruption and degradation among city police, prison guards, and even in the highly regimented military, requires quite a stretch of the imagination.

As borders are tightened, a black market in immigration will expand, leading to increased violence and government corruption. The war on drugs has utterly failed to keep drugs out of the country, and yet has succeeded in draining away enormous resources and eroding precious civil liberties; a war on immigrants would yield similar results.

For most of U.S. history, there were virtually no immigration controls.

Closed Immigration Is Unconstitutional

Moreover, just like all the other socialist federal programs in America, closed immigration is totally unconstitutional. Article I, Section 8, provides no authority whatever to the federal government to close the borders. It is a step in the wrong direction to violate the Constitution further, simply to allow one favored government program to slip through. Such leniency with the Constitution, after all, is how we wound up with so much socialism in the first place.

This brings us to the question of the history of immigration control. Many Americans point to the 1965 amendments to the Immigration Act, which loosened restrictions on immigration somewhat, and associate them with Lyndon Johnson's socialist Great Society programs of the same era, believing they are another indication that free immigration and socialism go hand in hand.

This does not necessarily follow any more than Andrew Jackson's opposition to central banking and his atrocious Trail of Tears, when taken together, demonstrate that free-market banking goes hand in hand with the brutal displacement of American Indians. Still, it is often useful to see the political movements associated with certain political trends and opinions.

In the case of immigration, we can go all the way back to the Declaration of Independence, in which Thomas Jefferson cited King George III's obstruction to immigration to the colonies as a grievance:

> He has endeavoured to prevent the Population of these States; for that Purpose obstructing the Laws for Naturalization of Foreigners; refusing to pass others to encourage their Migrations hither, and raising the Conditions of new Appropriations of Lands.

For most of U.S. history, there were virtually no immigration controls. Some northern states had Black Codes that kept free blacks from entering. Eventually, the federal government passed the Chinese Exclusion Act of 1882.

There was always a widespread movement to keep out the newest wave of immigrants, whether it was the Irish, the Chinese, the Japanese, Hispanics, or whomever. But it wasn't until the early 1920s that the United States imposed, and widely enforced, sweeping immigration legislation.

The Progressive Era and the Immigration Act of 1921

The early 1920s were a logical time for such legislation, for it was the tail end of what is called the Progressive Era. The progressives were a loose movement of Americans who advocated a hugely expansive and interventionist government, both at home and abroad. They championed electoral reform, business regulations, income taxation, and government-enforced personal morality. By the time the three presidents of the Progressive Era—Theodore Roosevelt, William Taft, and Woodrow Wilson—were done with their progressive reforms, America had seen the largest expansion in government power, and most significant shift in national politics, since the Civil War. Much of their agenda was accomplished in these three administrations—antitrust legislation, food and drug regulation, environmental "protection," a graduated income tax, central banking, and sweeping reforms in local political procedures.

The United States embarked for the first time on an imperialist foreign policy in 1898 with the Spanish American War, and the progressives continued this policy in Latin America and eventually in the nationalization of American industry and mobilization of millions of conscripts for U.S. entry into World War I.

The history of immigration in America coincides well with the history of liberty, and it shows the socialist origins of immigration controls.

The progressives also tended to believe in temperance, and they had a strong anti-immigrant streak. Their successes in these two arenas didn't come until the very end of the Progressive Era, with the alcohol prohibition of the Eighteenth Amendment and Volstead Act of 1920, and with the Immigration Act of 1921. The Republican administrations in the 1920s had some distinct differences from the progressives, but they implemented the policies on immigration and alcohol for which the progressives had fought for years.

Of course, the progressives were right once in a while, as on equal rights for women under the law. And the Great Society politicians in the 1960s were right once in a while, as in the relaxation of immigration controls in 1965.

But by and large, the Progressive movement was one of the most harmful episodes for American liberty and constitutionally limited government in U.S. history. It was an essentially socialist movement, and American progressives of the early 20th century understood the incompatibility between a free immigration policy and a managed economy, as well as the logical correlation between such an economy and immigration controls. Sometimes the progressives cloaked their advocacy for immigration controls under a guise of wanting to help the immigrants, but, as with their Progressive foreign policies, their humanitarian rhetoric about foreigners did not translate into genuine compassion in the real world.

Whereas many millions of immigrants came to America in the early 20th century, the decades that followed the passage of the Immigration Act of 1921 saw a severe decline in immigration. This was tragic for those who wanted to enter America, most notably when huddled masses of European Jews sought refuge from Hitler's terror but were denied entrance into the land of the free by Franklin Roosevelt, one of the most socialist presidents in American history.

The history of immigration in America coincides well with the history of liberty, and it shows the socialist origins of immigration controls. In its history, its theory, and its practice, immigration controls are just one more boondoggle of dysfunctional, immoral, unconstitutional, and socialist central planning. A welfare state may depend on such controls, but a free society should reject them. Severe restrictions on immigration compromise the liberty of the people inside as well as outside the borders, and they should be among the policies libertarians oppose in their efforts to bring liberty back to America.

7

The United States Should Not Adopt Open Immigration

Stephen Cox

Stephen Cox is editor of Liberty *magazine, a monthly libertarian review. Cox is also a professor of literature at the University of California, San Diego, as well as a successful nonfiction writer. Cox's books include* The Woman and the Dynamo: Isabel Paterson and the Idea of America *and* The Titanic Story: Hard Choices, Dangerous Decisions.

The supposed positive benefits of adopting open immigration in the United States are vastly outweighed by the negative effects that such a policy would bring. Most immigrants are not equal contributors to the U.S. economy. Illegal immigrants commonly do not pay taxes, and U.S. infrastructure will need tax money if it is to expand to take care of the influx of immigrants that result from an open-door policy. Immigrants almost always vote for liberal candidates, who in turn support funding and expanding government welfare programs—programs that strain government coffers. Some immigrants bring with them a history of criminal behavior, and some, even worse, a history of terrorism, in turn costing U.S. citizens more money. It is debatable whether people have a right to immigrate, but it is a nation's assured right to protect itself from those who could possibly harm it.

Few people want to keep foreign doctors, engineers, computer scientists, and financial magnates out of the United States. Most of the economic arguments for immigration are therefore defenses of immigration by poor and unskilled persons. Proponents of open borders insist that unskilled foreign workers contribute vastly more to the American economy than they cost, resting their case on the idea that "immigrants work hard and create wealth." Some also point out that a large supply of cheap labor makes the prices of certain other commodities cheaper, thereby making more money available for consumers to invest on other things, to the benefit of the whole economy. Others try to avoid that argument, for fear of alienating American workers who don't want their own wages to decline. These proponents bring forth a third argument: "Immigrants do work that Americans refuse to do."

Remember this argument the next time you watch your garbage being collected. Americans are perfectly willing to collect garbage. They are also perfectly willing to cook meals, prune flowers, or harvest vegetables—so long as someone is willing to pay them enough. If all immigration suddenly became legal, immigrants would enjoy the same wage scales as native-born workers. They would compete for the same jobs, join the same labor unions, and be subject to the same labor laws and the same rates of taxation as everybody else. In short, their wages would rise, and there would no longer be any work that "Americans won't do."

It is true, of course, that the existence of a large and growing supply of unskilled workers tends to reduce prices—especially the price of lawn mowing, Tyson's chicken, and certain kinds of fruits and vegetables. But if you think that the more unskilled laborers we have, the larger and more dynamic the economy will be, you have a strange idea about the production of wealth. When I have my car washed, some of the work is done by unskilled labor, but as much as possible is done by machines. If more human squirters and swabbers were available, I'm sure that the price of their labor would go down, and at some point the machines would be completely replaced by muscles. The same might be said about, say, the sweeping of streets or the growing of crops. I don't believe, however, that a low-wage, labor-intensive economy is preferable in any way to a machine economy, paying high wages to well-educated people. If you believe that, you belong in the pre-industrial age.

Despite all the talk about the economic contributions of unskilled labor, few unskilled immigrants contribute anything equal to what they extract from the unwilling taxpayer.

Recently the mayor of Los Angeles, trying to speak to America on behalf of all Mexican immigrants, shouted triumphantly to a rally of open-immigration supporters: "We [sic] cook your food! We [sic] clean your toilets!" People like the mayor are the last supporters of the labor theory of value. They think that wealth results automatically from toil. It doesn't. And great increases in wealth never do. They result from the kind of work that is done by people who are highly skilled and, ordinarily, highly paid. Our immigration policy should target the entrepreneurs, the professionals, the wealth producers, and make it easy for them to come to America—supposing, as I do, that doctors and software engineers do something more for the economy than the guys behind the counter of the local 7-11.

Immigrants Do Not Contribute Equally to the U.S. Economy

Do we have to choose the kind of workers who should be invited in? Yes, we do. I will return to that theme. Before doing so, I want to examine another issue that proponents of open borders usually don't want to think about: the net contributions of unskilled laborers to the *actual* American economy. Despite all the talk about the economic contributions of unskilled labor, few unskilled immigrants contribute anything equal to what they extract from the unwilling taxpayer.

I'm not saying this simply because illegal immigrants generally avoid paying income taxes. Imagine an unskilled laborer who has come here legally, just as proponents of open borders wish that all unskilled laborers could do. Let's say he makes $15,000 a year—an income that is above the minimum wage, an income that is quite good enough to draw millions of people here from almost anywhere in the world, provided we had open borders. And let's say that his wife works too (part time, because of the kids) and makes $10,000 a year. That $25,000 is the value they contribute to the American economy. Out of it, they pay maybe $1,200 in sales taxes, $500 in the property taxes that are included in their rent, $1,900 in Social Security payments, and zip in income taxes. (Whatever taxes are extracted from their checks, they get back in refunds. Actually, because of tax subsidies to poor people, they will probably get back a good deal more than they pay in, but to be extra-fair I won't pause to calculate that.)

Of course, the Social Security contributions are not invested and will never earn enough to pay the total cost of the couple's retirement benefits; other taxpayers will have to do that. In this respect, the couple is already a serious economic loss. The scale of that loss will appear when they retire. Other losses are happening right now. Because of their low income, man and wife are eligible for innumerable welfare programs—from subsidized housing to medical assistance (if they don't have adequate private insurance, which they won't) to free legal aid to disaster aid if a storm comes through. Any physical disability may result in hundreds of thousands of dollars in bills to other taxpayers. Whenever the couple have a child, that's $10,000 at the county hospital. Afterwards, it's probably $5,000 a year for a government-financed preschool, then $10,000 a year (the approximate national average) in government funds for K–12 education.

Let's not even think about the public bills for their children's college education. Or—to look at the other side of the coin—for the social problems of a population in which relatively few people qualify for a college education. Some of those problems were pointed out by Heather MacDonald in an article in the Summer 2006 *City Journal* [a New York City urban policy magazine]. She noted that in 2002 half the Hispanic children born in the United States were born out of wedlock. Further, "The illegitimacy rate in Mexico is 38 percent; in El Salvador, it is 72 percent." Immigration from these countries currently seems to select for "social choices" that are detrimental to society.

But to return. Suppose that our unskilled couple has three children. This family is putting $25,000 into the economy, taking $30,000 out of it, *just for K–12 education* ($54,000, if they live in Los Angeles), and paying only about $3,600 in taxes. Oh, but there are other things. Dwellers in the city of Los Angeles sop up about $2,500 per year, per capita, in city and county expenditures for . . . this and that. Now the five-member family, if located in Los Angeles or some other large city, is putting $25,000 into the economy and extracting $42,500 (and more, much more, that I haven't tried to quantify). Net cost to other taxpayers, once the family's own tax contribution is figured in: $38,900.

Poor people, and ethnically self-identified recent immigrants vote overwhelmingly for modern-liberal candidates.

I haven't even mentioned the cost of new highways, airports, and rapid transit, or anything else constructed by state and federal governments to minister to America's burgeoning population. Shall I add the increased cost of car insurance resulting from an influx of people who are too poor to buy it for themselves? Or the increasing expenditures for security guards and other crime-protection devices in neighborhoods inundated by unskilled, unassimilated poor folk? Or the rising costs of homes in the places to which former residents of those neighborhoods flee? Or the increased costs of controlling the formerly obscure diseases now coursing across our frontiers from every economically backward area of the world?

The Immigrant Vote

But the best part is yet to come. Poor people, and ethnically self-identified recent immigrants vote overwhelmingly for modern-liberal candidates [as opposed to classical liberal, also known as libertarian], and modern-liberal candidates, once elected, take as the whole duty of life the effort to raise taxes and expand government programs and entitlements. They seek to bless their constituency with affirmative action programs, ethnic quotas, foreign-language maintenance programs, socialist and race-conscious school curricula, and every other modern-liberal institution that has any potential for transforming the United States into the Canadian or Mexican version of a progressive country.

The expectation of political support explains why modern-liberal politicians are such vigorous proponents of immigration, why they are, even now, trying to enlist illegal immigrants in the electoral process. . . . The same goes for labor unions. They used to be the biggest opponents of immigration. No more. Now most of them are endorsing every open-borders proposal that comes along. Why? Because they too have identified their natural constituency: unskilled, politically unsophisticated workers, just waiting to be organized in support of higher minimum-wage laws, universal social welfare, and whatever other political demands the unions want to make.

Is it possible that politicians and labor leaders know a few things that libertarian theorists don't? Is it possible that they

have correctly identified the current immigration from third-world countries as the ultimate weapon in the attack on limited government?

Nor is this mere politics, without any economic implications. Suppose, as frequently happens, that an election in the state of California results in a modest increase of one billion dollars in state expenditures, and that the election is won by a margin of 100,000 votes. Every voter within that margin has just cost the taxpayers one billion dollars, or $10,000 per left-wing voter. One would think that libertarians would do everything they could to decrease that margin. Instead, many libertarians, even candidates of the Libertarian Party, join with labor unions, Mexican nationalists, the hierarchy of the Roman Catholic church, professional advocates of the welfare state, and [George W.] Bushite conservatives, hustling for any vote they think they can get, in attempting to *increase* the number of voters who are likely to approve the largest possible extension of the welfare state.

This would be funny, if it were happening on some other planet.

We do know that every one of the 9/11 terrorists was an alien, and that several of them were illegal aliens.

Immigrants Bring Crime

But thus far, we've been considering only the people who cross America's borders with the honorable intention of working and supporting themselves, whether they actually manage to do so or not. This is the only group that open-border advocates want to notice. Yet there are other immigrants—lots of them. There are (1) the tens of millions of nonworking relatives of the already-immigrated, tens of millions of people whom a liberalized immigration policy would bring to this

country under the aegis of "family unification"; (2) the criminal class that is already migrated here in enormous numbers; and (3) quite simply, terrorists.

No one can say how many people are included in the first group, though the number is certainly stupendous. As for the second group, testimony submitted in 2005 to a committee of the House of Representatives by Richard Stana, Director of Homeland Security [and Justice Issues at the Government Accounting Office], reveals that at the end of 2004 there were 49,000 criminal aliens in federal prisons (15% more than at the end of 2001). Stana—with every sign of unwillingness, employed as he is by the [George W.] Bush administration—also revealed the existence of 215,000 other criminal aliens for whose incarceration the federal government reimbursed state and local governments during fiscal year 2002 ("data represent only a portion of the population"). Those, of course, are the few people who got caught. Let's make a conservative estimate of the costs of their imprisonment (not of their crimes), and put the bill at about $13,000,000,000. That is one of the small, ancillary, foot-notable costs of uncontrolled immigration.

Terrorism can also be an economic problem. A single terrorist attack can easily cost this country tens or even hundreds of billions of dollars. Which do you think is likelier to reduce the risk of terrorist penetration of America—making it easier to get into the country, or harder?

We do not know how many intended terrorists have been turned back at our borders. We do know that every one of the 9/11 [2001] terrorists was an alien, and that several of them were illegal aliens. And evidence of bad intentions never ceases to appear. Last month [September 2006] an example appeared in the government's special green-card program for religious workers. *The Boston Globe*—not exactly an anti-immigrant venue—obtained a copy of Homeland Security's hitherto secret study of the program. It showed that one-third of visa applications were fraudulent, and "instances of fraud were

particularly high among applicants from predominantly Muslim countries." Clearly, it is not in the interest of the people of the United States to permit unlimited immigration of clerics from Arabia or unemployed young men from Egypt, no matter how much money they bring with them. But under the principle of open immigration, in they come.

In my experience, proponents of open immigration rarely stay to listen to arguments like the ones I've just tried to outline. If they do, they ordinarily drop their own economic argument and turn to the moral argument about human rights. So . . .

The "Right" to Immigrate

In a way, it's silly to argue against the "right" to immigrate. Very few open-borders people actually believe in it. When questioned about who should be allowed to take up residence here, they almost always say, "Oh, everyone—everyone, that is, who will swear to support the Constitution," or "Everyone—everyone, that is, who is willing to work for a living," or even, with President [George W.] Bush, "Everyone—everyone, that is, who . . . who is a . . . who is a decent person and . . . uh . . . wants, who wants to learn English." Thus they admit that the "right" to immigrate is no right at all.

My right to freedom of speech is in no way contingent on the language I speak, on my possession of a job, or on my willingness to give a political oath. A right is absolute. It is conditioned by nothing. It depends on no action of mine. It is endowed by my Creator. It is inalienable. But advocates of the "right" to immigrate see this "right" as far from absolute, unconditioned, or inalienable. They make it dependent on something else. They call it a right, but they don't believe that it is one, any more than I do.

If you say that any country in the world that wants to get rid of its convicts and insane asylum inmates can send them to the United States, as Cuba did in 1980, and the United

States is morally obliged to take them in, because they have a right to be here, then I will admit that you are talking about people's *right* to immigrate.

If you say that you welcome the idea of a hundred thousand Wahhabi missionaries being allowed to land in America, with no attempt to check or approve them in any way, and with no regard to their political affiliations or intentions, then I will admit that you are talking about people's *right* to immigrate.

If you say that any nut-ball political or religious group has the right to import its adherents, by the tens or hundreds of thousands, with the intention of supporting them on public welfare until such time as they are ready to bomb Wal-Marts all over Kansas and Missouri, then I will admit that you believe in people's *right* to immigrate.

But if you say that you welcome the idea of ten million more unskilled laborers arriving from Mexico, because that is their right, except that they should not be permitted to live here unless they get a job, learn English, and swear to support the Constitution, then you're not talking about a right at all. You're just talking about something that you want to happen.

So much, I might conclude, for the issue of rights. Even the proponents of immigration "rights" don't really take them seriously. But why do people think they do? That's a more interesting question. In my view, it's because of an understandable confusion between the right to immigrate and the right to emigrate.

Can the people living in a nation properly decide to keep other people out of it, as a householder might decide to keep strangers out of his bungalow? . . . Yes they can.

How many times have you heard somebody bewail the perfectly practical idea of building a fence or "wall" along our frontiers? "It's just like the Berlin Wall!" they cry. Now, before you say, "That's the silliest analogy I've ever heard—the Berlin

Wall was meant to keep people *in* their own country, not *out* of somebody else's!" you should grant the fact that immigration and emigration are, from a purely factual or photographic point of view, the same thing. Every act of immigration is necessarily an act of emigration. If you took a picture of [al Qaeda terrorist leader] Osama bin Laden leaving Quebec, it would be the same picture as one of Osama bin Laden entering New Hampshire.

But the philosophical as well as the practical difference is immense. Jason quarrels with Joanna and walks out of their house. Jason has a perfect right to leave. But he does not have a right to leave for *my house*, despite the fact that his leaving her and his coming to me are, to all appearances, the same act. Someone's right to leave East Germany did not entail that person's right to turn up in the United States, Bulgaria, Burundi, or even West Germany. It was simply the right to leave East Germany. If your house burns down, and I am next door to you, you do not have a *right* to come and live in my house. I may let you live there. More likely, I will let you visit. This might be a good idea, but it's up to me. It's not *your right*.

Well . . . but . . . is a nation really like a house? Can the people living in a nation properly decide to keep other people out of it, as a householder might decide to keep strangers out of his bungalow? Yes it is, and yes they can.

America Must Have Security and Freedom

A nation's laws and customs are the framework in which its people live their lives. Life involves enormous investment of time and effort. It requires a framework. It requires stability. It requires a certain amount of predictability. It requires the ability to say, well, I will buy a home in Hillcrest—without worrying about the possibility that Hillcrest may soon be overwhelmed by immigrants from some Islamic country who decide to ban homosexuality, pork, the Episcopal Church, and slacks on women.

Human life also requires freedom as well as stability—and the more the better, so far as I'm concerned. A real nation is not a prison; but it isn't a tent, either. It isn't something that is constantly being changed and moved. To build a decent house, to make sure that it doesn't collapse like a tent or constrain like a prison, requires an even greater investment than the other projects of human life. It requires an investment in cooperation, self-restraint, commitment to constitutional order, long-continued belief in first principles. A house whose door is always open, a house where everybody has the right to enter, have a good meal, do a little work around the place, and by virtue of his residence, or mere visitation, start remodeling the structure, regardless of its original plan—that is no longer a house. At best, it's a squatters' camp, where anything may happen, as in the squatters' camps that illegal immigrants have erected all over the American Southwest, defying property owners to do anything about it.

To the degree that a nation is like a house, and requires the security of a house, its inhabitants must have the ability to decide whom they wish to invite inside, whom they wish to enjoy the many investments already made in it. If the house is designed to protect individual liberty, its maintenance requires the exclusion of people whose ill-advised decisions might endanger liberty's protective mechanisms.

No one has the right to move to a free country and destroy its freedom. But this is precisely what happens when people who are unused to the political culture of individual liberty, or who disapprove of it, swing the balance of national decisions.

8

A Border Fence Will Reduce Illegal Crossings of the U.S.–Mexico Border

Ronald D. Vitiello

Ronald D. Vitiello is a chief patrol agent for the U.S. Border Patrol's Rio Grande Valley Sector.

The U.S. Border Patrol, part of the Department of Homeland Security, is responsible for monitoring U.S. borders and apprehending those that would seek to enter the United States illegally. Along the nation's southern border, Border Patrol agents seize thousands of illegal aliens every year and deter many more from making the crossing from Mexico into the United States. One of the most important tools the Border Patrol has in carrying out its mission is the miles of pedestrian and vehicle fencing that stretches across several major points of entry. To aid the Border Patrol and ensure that it can fulfill its mandate, the government should expedite the extension of border fences to cut off other crossing sites. Taking into account the environmental impact and the concerns of local residents, the construction of new fences can be accomplished to meet Border Patrol objectives without jeopardizing the resources and natural beauty of these border regions.

U.S. Customs and Border Protection (CBP) is responsible for protecting more than 4,000 miles of border with Canada, 1,900 miles of border with Mexico, and 2,627 miles

Ronald D. Vitiello, "Walls and Waivers: Expedited Construction of the Southern Border Wall and Collateral Impacts to Communities and the Environment," Statement Before the House Committee on Natural Resources, Subcommittee on National Parks, Forests and Public Lands, Subcommittee on Fish, Wildlife and Oceans, April 28, 2008.

of coastal border to include the island of Puerto Rico. The U.S. Border Patrol is the sole entity responsible for securing our Nation's borders between the official ports of entry and bases its operation on the Border Patrol National Strategy. To that end, our objectives are to apprehend terrorists and terrorist weapons illegally entering the United States; to deter entries through improved enforcement; detect, apprehend and deter smugglers of humans, drugs, and other contraband; and to improve the quality of life in border communities. The Border Patrol uses a combination of efforts in achieving our goals. The Border Patrol depends on a 'defense in depth' posture, utilizing agents in the field, interior immigration checkpoints, and coordinated enforcement operations, as well as partnerships with other federal and state law enforcement agencies.

During Fiscal Year (FY) 2007 alone, Border Patrol agents apprehended 876,704 persons (858,638 on the southwest border) attempting to enter the United States illegally, including human smugglers, drug traffickers, and illegal aliens, and seized 1,859,299 pounds of marijuana and 14,242 pounds of cocaine. As of April 20, 2008, in FY2008, the Border Patrol has arrested 422,433 illegal aliens (411,329 on the southwest border) and seized 952,847 pounds of marijuana and 6,625 pounds of cocaine. In my area of responsibility, the Rio Grande Valley Sector, in FY2008 alone we have apprehended 42,004 illegal aliens and seized 189,377 pounds of marijuana and 3,461 pounds of cocaine.

Various Methods Are Needed to Secure the Borders

Securing our Nation's diverse border terrain is an important and complex task that cannot be resolved by a single solution alone. To secure each unique mile of the border requires a balance of personnel, technology, and tactical infrastructure (such as roads, pedestrian and vehicle fencing, and lights) that is tailored to each specific environment. The installation of fencing has proven to be an effective tool to slow, redirect, and deter illegal entries, especially in certain areas where personnel and technology alone cannot sufficiently secure the border.

For example, in an urban environment, an illegal entrant can be across the border and into the community in a matter of minutes, sometimes seconds. In this environment, fencing provides a critical barrier. In a rural environment agents have more time to bring an illegal incursion to the proper resolution, making it more likely that vehicles will be used as a conveyance for getting from the point of entry to staging areas and community infrastructure that supports them. In this environment, vehicle fence can be utilized to prevent vehicles from entering and limit the speed and carrying capability of illegal entrants, along with sensor and surveillance technology to detect and track illegal entrants on foot. Remote areas may be completely uninhabited with no roads at or near the border. It could take someone hours or even days to be able to cross the border and get to a road or community infrastructure. Vehicle fence could be applied to remote areas where a vehicle could travel cross-country.

The effectiveness of tactical infrastructure can be seen in the 14-mile congressionally mandated fence in San Diego, California, which, in combination with increased personnel and technology, has proved effective in reducing the number of apprehensions made in the San Diego Sector. Over a 12-year period between 1992 and 2004, overall apprehensions made in the San Diego Sector declined by 76 percent. The Imperial Beach and Chula Vista Stations, whose areas of responsibilities fall within the 14-mile project area, combined for 361,125 apprehensions in 1992. By 2004, total apprehensions in these two stations dropped to 19,038 as a result of the increase in fencing, manpower, and technology.

In the Yuma [Arizona] Sector during the same 12-year period, apprehensions increased by 591 percent. More recently, however, no sector has seen a bigger decrease in apprehensions and vehicle drive-throughs. With the addition of tactical infrastructure and increased staffing over the past two years, apprehensions in the Yuma Sector in FY2007 decreased by 68 percent and are down 76 percent to date in FY2008. Vehicle drive-through traffic within the Barry M. Goldwater Range (BMGR) decreased from 694 in FY2006 to 251 in FY2007 and 150 in FY2008 (all statistics covering only the timeframe between October 1 and April 3 of the given fiscal year). Vehicle drive-through activity elsewhere within the Yuma Sector during the same time period decreased from 423 in FY2006 to 145 in FY2007 and 0 in FY2008.

In Rio Grande Valley Sector, I identified approximately 70 miles of border on which pedestrian fencing is operationally necessary to gain effective control of the border.

The Border Fence Has Congressional Support

In fact, Congress recognized that tactical infrastructure is critical to securing the Nation's borders by mandating that the Department of Homeland Security (DHS) "achieve and maintain" operational control of the border and requiring DHS to construct—in the most expeditious manner possible—the infrastructure necessary to deter and prevent illegal entry. DHS is responding to this mandate and installing fencing, barriers, roads, lighting, cameras, and sensors on hundreds of miles of the southwest border. DHS will have 670 miles of pedestrian and vehicle fencing completed by the end of December 2008. These priority miles of fencing are to be constructed in areas where fencing would be most practical and effective in deterring smugglers and aliens attempting to gain illegal entry into the United States.

Operational assessments by the local Border Patrol agents and Chiefs—based on illegal cross-border activity and the Border Patrol's extensive field experience—identified multiple locations where fencing would most effectively enhance border security. These operational assessments identified approximately 370 miles of pedestrian fencing. In Rio Grande Valley Sector, I identified approximately 70 miles of border on which pedestrian fencing is operationally necessary to gain effective control of the border, and my fellow Sector Chiefs performed these same assessments in their areas of operation.

In addition to the Border Patrol's operational assessments, several other factors contribute to decisions to construct tactical infrastructure in certain locations, including engineering assessments, which include the cost to construct; environmental assessments; and input from state and local stakeholders, including landowners. Each of these steps is a standard element of the planning process that enables us to make informed decisions in deploying the right mix of tactical infrastructure.

The Department of Homeland Security's Commitment

As noted earlier, to meet our operational goals, DHS is committed to building a total of 370 miles of pedestrian fence and 300 miles of vehicle fence along the southwest border by the end of December 2008. In a letter to [DHS] Secretary [Michael] Chertoff on March 20, 2008, Associate Deputy Secretary of the Interior James Cason informed him that while Department of the Interior (DOI) managers were attempting to facilitate the construction of border infrastructure on federal land, they had come to realize DOI could not accommodate approval of some tactical infrastructure projects based on legal obligations.

Given these obstacles and the ambitious timeline for a project of this scope and scale, on April 1, 2008, Secretary

Chertoff determined that it was necessary to utilize the authority given to him by Congress to waive any legal requirements he determined necessary to ensure the expeditious construction of infrastructure needed to secure the border. Absent the Secretary's use of the waiver authority, it would not be possible to achieve the objectives set forth. The first waiver applies to certain environmental and land management laws for various project areas along the southwest border, encompassing roughly 470 total miles. The waiver will facilitate additional pedestrian and vehicle fence construction, towers, sensors, cameras, detection equipment, and roads in the vicinity of the border. The second waiver was signed for the levee-border barrier project in Hidalgo County, Texas. This roughly 22-mile project will strengthen flood protection in the area while providing the Border Patrol with important tactical infrastructure. In addition to environmental and land management laws, this waiver addresses other legal and administrative impediments to completing this project by the end of the calendar year.

In planning for a project of this magnitude, DHS cannot anticipate every potential legal impediment that may arise during construction. Accordingly, each law listed in the waivers was either an immediate impediment to expeditious construction or was determined to be a potential source of administrative delay or litigation. As Secretary Chertoff stated in his April 1, 2008, press release concerning the waiver, "criminal activity at the border does not stop for endless debate or protracted litigation."

Minimizing Environmental Impact

However, the Secretary's decision to invoke his waiver authority does not mean that CBP has turned its back on environmental stewardship or continued consultation with stakeholders who will be directly affected by the construction of new border infrastructure. We will continue to coordinate closely with the federal land managers to ensure impacts to the environment, wildlife, and cultural and historic artifacts are minimized to the fullest extent practicable.

The flow of illegal pedestrian and vehicle traffic across the border not only jeopardizes our ability to secure our borders, but it has also caused severe and profound impacts to the environment.

As an example of our commitment to the environment, U.S. Fish and Wildlife Service (USFWS) representatives participated in the first comprehensive review of the proposed fence alignment in the Rio Grande Valley in September 2007. USFWS provided comments on each fence section and made suggestions, where necessary, relative to fence realignments that would substantially reduce potential impacts to threatened and endangered species, or would impact components of the Lower Rio Grande Valley National Wildlife Refuge and nature reserves in the region. Throughout the planning process, the USFWS has continued to provide advice on the fence types and alignment of the fence project segments, including input regarding incorporating cat passages into the fence in specific areas that have the potential to serve as movement corridors for the ocelot and jaguarondi.

It is important to note that the flow of illegal pedestrian and vehicle traffic across the border not only jeopardizes our ability to secure our borders, but it has also caused severe and profound impacts to the environment. For example, illegal roads divert the normal flow of water and rob native plant cover of the moisture it depends on to survive. Illegal entrants also leave trash and high concentrations of human waste, which impact wildlife, vegetation, and water quality. Numerous wildfires caused by campfires of illegal entrants have caused a significant threat to human safety and the lands along the border, as well as increased impacts to soil, vegetation, cultural sites, and other sensitive resources. We believe that efforts to stem illegal cross border activity in certain areas of high traffic will result in an improvement to the environment and increase the public's ability to enjoy it as a resource.

Listening to Local Inhabitants

In addition to our commitment to responsible environmental stewardship, CBP continues to solicit and respond to the needs of state, local, and tribal governments, other agencies of the federal government, and local residents. CBP has gone to great lengths to obtain public input throughout our planning efforts regarding the construction of fence along the southwest border. CBP has engaged in extensive discussions about the placement of fencing with state and local stakeholders, including repeated consultations with landowners. CBP has contacted more than 600 different landowners, hosted 11 public open houses, held 15 publicly-advertised town hall meetings, and conducted 84 meetings with state and local officials and public groups.

The Border Patrol's objective is nothing less than securing operational control of the border.

As a result of these outreach efforts, there are many instances where we were able to make modifications to our original plans to accommodate landowner/community concerns while still meeting our operational needs. For example, we made numerous alignment changes to the Rio Grande Valley segments to limit impacts to the USFWS National Wildlife Refuge areas, a bird watching observation facility in the City of Roma, and negate the need to relocate approximately 30 residences. The fence alignment at the Roma Port of Entry (POE) was initially proposed to be on top of a 30-foot bluff. During our site visit in September, it was determined that placing the fence at the top of the bluff would impact historical buildings and bring about constructability issues. Based on these findings, Border Patrol, U.S. Army Corps of Engineers, and USFWS came to a compromise to construct the fence at the bottom of the bluff, where it would still provide operational utility. We will continue to consult with our state and local stakeholders, including landowners, to ensure that our investments effectively balance border security with the diverse needs of those that live in border communities.

The Border Patrol's objective is nothing less than securing operational control of the border. We recognize the challenges of doing so, as we have dealt with them for many years. Challenges continue to lie ahead and the need for a comprehensive enforcement approach remains. Our national strategy gives us the means by which to achieve our ambitious goal. We face these challenges every day with vigilance, dedication to service, and integrity as we work to strengthen national security and protect America and its citizens.

9

A Border Fence Will Not Reduce Illegal Crossings of the U.S.–Mexico Border

Daniel B. Wood

Daniel B. Wood is a staff writer for the Christian Science Monitor.

The 2006 Secure Fence Act envisioned 700 miles of fencing along the U.S.–Mexico border, but many people are unconvinced the fence will actually stop illegal immigrants from crossing the border. Some local residents near the border don't need to be persuaded the fence isn't working; they see illegal immigrants crossing their farms every day. Mounting costs have led to a patchwork fence made up of various leftover materials, which the Border Patrol says saves money and is still effective, but others point to this as another reason building a fence on the border is not practical.

After driving 10 miles along the expanded US–Mexican border fence near her farm, Dawn Garner offers her dour assessment: "Anyone can plainly see this wouldn't stop a flea, let alone a migrant or terrorist."

A jagged patchwork of metal mesh, corrugated steel, vertical bollards, chest-high railroad rails, and waist-high barbed wire has been cobbled together along the southern border east of Naco [Arizona] by various National Guard units over the

Daniel B. Wood, "Along U.S.–Mexican Border, an Erratic Patchwork Fence," *Christian Science Monitor*, April 3, 2008.

past summer. Hard-hatted workers from a general contractor, Sundt Inc., continue to dig ditches and grade terrain across plains of fluorescent-green prairie grass framed by saw-toothed mountains.

"This [fence] is just too easy to cut into, climb over, or go under or around," says Ms. Garner. Twenty to 40 illegal migrant workers cut across her five-acre farm daily, she says.

Unlike in San Luis, Ariz., and San Diego, where double-and-triple metal walls are backed by lighting and cameras, the fencing being built along this part of the US–Mexican border is piecemeal. Such a fence is pointless, say local ranchers.

The border patrol, however, contends that it is cost-effective, and more potent than it seems.

A Mishmash of Materials

Here in Naco, the wall is being built on mostly federally owned land. So there is little of the outrage over fair compensation and invasion of private property as there is in Texas, or complaints about cutting landowners off from land that falls on the Mexican side of the wall, as in the Tohono O'odham Indian Reservation to the west.

The fence is made of steel girders pounded into the ground vertically, with some laid across at waist height—able to stop cars but easy for people to step over or crawl under.

Neither has there been as much ecological concern as farther north near San Pedro—though this may change, as the Department of Homeland Security announced it would waive certain environmental and land rules for 470 miles of the border from California to Texas and another 22 miles in Hidalgo County, Tex.

Rather, most local residents seem concerned about building a wall that actually stops illegal immigrants.

"We don't want a Berlin Wall or anything, just something that keeps migrants from flooding our backyards," says Garner, accelerating her bright yellow Jeep down the gravel road that runs alongside the newly built fencing stretching east from the tiny border crossing at Naco toward New Mexico.

As Garner drives, an eclectic array of fence styles and materials flutter by in the bright sun.

One stretch of the fence is made of a kind of steel, Vietnam-era material—once used as landing mats for helicopters touching down on the jungle floor—held together vertically by steel girders. Another stretch of the fence comprises corrugated steel bars placed one on top of the other to a height of 10 feet, and capped by another three feet of metal mesh.

A third style is built of staggered, cylindrical pillars known as bollards, with just enough of a crack between them to allow small rodents or birds through—but not humans.

As the landscape turns desolate and the terrain rough, the fencing alters even more. In some places are vertical metal slats that look like suburban picket fences, only higher. In others, the fence is made of steel girders pounded into the ground vertically, with some laid across at waist height—able to stop cars but easy for people to step over or crawl under.

This patchwork fence is interspersed with 100-yard gaps where there's no barrier at all or traditional barbed-wire fencing.

Out in the desert, "vehicle barriers" begin to appear, made of used railway rails that resemble Abe Lincoln–era split-rail fences. "Well, these are sturdier than they look and it seems they would stop a car," acknowledges Garner. "But as you can see, anyone in a car could simply drive around one of these."

An Excuse for a Wall?

Ranchers here say they don't understand the logic behind the eclectic potpourri of fence styles. It's just politics, says Richard

Hodges, owner of a 372-acre cattle ranch whose family has lived here since homestead days. "[It's] because they need to say they got a wall up."

But the US border patrol says a patchwork wall isn't as bad as it seems. Using leftover materials means huge savings, agents say. Funding for the original 700-mile fence envisioned by the 2006 Secure Fence Act was about $1.2 billion. Only $200 million has been spent so far and the goal has been scaled back some, but there is still more than 370 miles of fence to be built by the end of 2008.

Costs have been mounting—a mile of metal fencing costs $3 million to $4 million, according to border patrol—and include putting up National Guard troops in local hotels.

The patchwork barrier reflects the impracticality of border fencing, say some observers.

Border patrol officials say that in places like Naco, it is not necessary to build an impenetrable fence. "In urban areas like San Diego, once a migrant jumps the fence, he has only a few yards to disappear into the city," says Mike Scioli of the Tucson Sector Border Patrol. "But down here, we only need to slow them down."

Using mesh and bollard allows the border patrol to see through to the Mexican side of the fence—a critical tactical ploy that allows agents to see someone trying to cut or torch through from the other side, Mr. Scioli says. Also, in the cat-and-mouse games that occur daily in these areas, an eclectic fence forces illegal migrants to choose a section of fence to climb over, dig under, or cut through. Then, when border patrol agents chase them back, they have to find the exact hole they came through—making them easier to catch.

Still, not everyone is convinced. The patchwork barrier reflects the impracticality of border fencing, say some observers. "The nation is caught between the forces saying something must be done and the practicalities that it can't properly be executed," says Patricia Hamm, assistant professor of political science at Iowa State University. "And so we end up with what we've got—so many miles of wall that officials can point to from Washington [DC] to say 'We've done it.' And local residents and others who see what's in front of them say, 'It doesn't matter, it won't work.'"

10

A Border Fence Will Harm the Environment

Glenn Hurowitz

Glenn Hurowitz is the president of Democratic Courage, a progressive political action committee based in Washington, D.C. Hurowitz is also the author of the 2007 book Fear and Courage in the Democratic Party *and is a contributor to the* American Prospect *and the* Huffington Post.

The expansion of the border fence between Mexico and the United States would destroy desert ecosystems and disrupt the migratory patterns of animals that cross the border to hunt and breed. In addition, parts of a legislative deal involving the lengthening of the fence would grant legal status to immigrants already in the United States, encouraging others to flood into the country. This huge number of people would lead to greater fuel consumption and other negative environmental impacts that result from the U.S. consumerist lifestyle.

The biggest—and least talked about—loser in the immigration "grand bargain" announced last week [in May 2007] is the planet. The deal amounts to an environmental double-whammy: If enacted, it would cause damage through those provisions meant to increase the number of immigrants in this country and through those designed to keep immigrants out.

The legislation requires the construction of 370 miles of border fencing before any liberalizing of immigration is al-

Glenn Hurowitz, "Deal on Immigration Threatens Environment," *Baltimore Sun*, May 22, 2007.

lowed to go forward. But this is no white picket fence between friendly neighbors. Instead, it's a double-layered concrete barrier more than 10 feet high—a little taste of Cold War Berlin on the Rio Grande. To build it, contractors would have to clear a 150-foot-wide swath of delicate desert ecosystem to allow the Border Patrol's trucks to cruise between the two walls, looking for traces of particularly stupid immigrants—those who for some reason decide not to simply go around.

It wouldn't just be an eyesore, either. The wall would sunder several wildlife refuges that provide vital habitat for the fragile fauna of the desert Southwest and that local conservationists have worked for years to establish.

Affected Species

Jaguars have recently returned to these refuges from Mexico after being hunted to extinction here decades ago. But the great cats' recovery is precarious, and they still need to interact with Mexican breeding populations to perpetuate the species—interaction that would be cut off by the wall.

Immigrants aren't to blame for the environmental harm caused by the American lifestyle. They're not the ones who created it; they're just participating in it.

The Sonoran pronghorn antelope is another species likely to be doomed by the wall. In 2002, increasingly intense border activity, possibly combined with the effects of global warming, caused the pronghorn's U.S. population to collapse to 21. If a wall cuts off this remnant population from the Mexican pronghorns in the El Pinacate Biosphere Reservc to the south, it could be the last nail in the coffin for this natural wonder, a subspecies of the fastest land animal in the Western Hemisphere.

Given the threats, the Endangered Species Act normally would prevent the construction of a wall and require consideration of alternatives such as further increasing the number of Border Patrol agents, installing more nondestructive vehicle barriers, and making greater use of electronic surveillance technology. But early this year, the [George W.] Bush administration waived all environmental laws for the area.

A Flood of Immigrants Would Further Harm the Environment

The border region would be just the first among many communities that would suffer environmental damage from this deal. By giving legal status to most of the 12 million undocumented workers in the country, the deal sends a clear message to people thinking about coming to the United States: Enter illegally and you'll eventually be allowed to stay.

That's likely to produce another flood of immigration from countries in Latin America and Asia with relatively low consumption levels. But when those immigrants and their descendants move to the United States, their lifestyles (and especially those of their children) often change, and their greenhouse-gas emissions skyrocket. Many start driving huge SUVs [sport utility vehicles] and living in big American houses in the suburbs, with air conditioning blasting. Of course, immigrants aren't to blame for the environmental harm caused by the American lifestyle. They're not the ones who created it; they're just participating in it. Nevertheless, the population surge this bill encourages would be likely to wipe out many of the environmental gains from global warming legislation under consideration by Congress.

The guest-worker provisions of the deal would exacerbate those environmental effects by preventing many immigrants who do come to this country from becoming citizens. While that's offensive from a human rights perspective, it's likely to be just as damaging for the environment. Historically, employers have taken advantage of immigrant workers and subjected them to extremely hazardous working conditions that citizens wouldn't tolerate. Agribusiness in particular is notorious for exposing immigrants to toxic pesticides. Politically, the prohibitions on citizenship for guest workers would allow industry to take advantage of immigrant workers without having to contend with a political backlash.

Environmentalists Need to Take Action

Part of the reason senators concluded a deal so damaging to the environment was that national environmental groups largely sat out the debate. The issue has historically divided the environmental movement between those who sympathize with immigrants' hunger for a better life and activists for whom environmental concerns always come first. Environmental leaders are wary of reigniting those battles. With almost no one pressing them on the issue, the senators who negotiated this deal were all too happy to let environmental concerns slide.

But as the extent of the environmental damage becomes clear, ignoring immigration's effects can no longer be an option. Environmentalists will have to work out their differences—or risk seeing much of their good work in other areas undone.

In this case, that means insisting on a just immigration policy that does not come at the expense of the natural environment that all of us—citizen and noncitizen, immigrant and native-born—are entrusted to protect.

11

A Border Fence Will Harm Poor U.S. Citizens

Melissa del Bosque

Melissa del Bosque is an investigative reporter for the progressive-left Texas [Austin] Observer.

To build a wall to secure the U.S.–Mexico border, the government is appropriating land on which to erect the structure. However, residents are complaining the land under consideration is almost always occupied by poor and modest-income homeowners; private clubs and wealthy citizens are seemingly exempt from the intrusion of the wall. Corporations who stand to profit from the building of the fence are lining the pockets of legislators responsible for granting contracts and passing pro-fence legislation, while poor citizens watch as their families' lands disappear at the hands of the U.S. government.

As the U.S. Department of Homeland Security [DHS] marches down the Texas border serving condemnation lawsuits to frightened landowners, Brownsville resident Eloisa Tamez, 72, has one simple question. She would like to know why her land is being targeted for destruction by a border wall, while a nearby golf course and resort remain untouched.

Tamez, a nursing director at the University of Texas at Brownsville, is one of the last of the Spanish land grant heirs in Cameron County. Her ancestors once owned 12,000 acres. In the 1930s, the federal government took more than half of her inherited land, without paying a cent, to build flood levees.

Melissa del Bosque, "Holes in the Wall," *Texas Observer*, February 22, 2008. Reproduced by permission.

Now Homeland Security wants to put an 18-foot steel and concrete wall through what remains. While the border wall will go through her backyard and effectively destroy her home, it will stop at the edge of the River Bend Resort and golf course, a popular Winter Texan [people who live in Texas in the winter] retreat two miles down the road. The wall starts up again on the other side of the resort.

"It has a golf course and all of the amenities," Tamez says. "There are no plans to build a wall there. If the wall is so important for security, then why are we skipping parts?"

Along the border, preliminary plans for fencing seem to target landowners of modest means and cities and public institutions such as the University of Texas at Brownsville, which rely on the federal government to pay their bills.

A visit to the River Bend Resort in late January [2008] reveals row after row of RVs [recreational vehicles] and trailers with license plates from chilly northern U.S. states and Canadian provinces. At the edge of a lush, green golf course, a Winter Texan from Canada enjoys the mild, South Texas winter and the landscaped ponds, where white egrets pause to contemplate golf carts whizzing past. The woman, who declines to give her name, recounts that illegal immigrants had crossed the golf course once while she was teeing off. They were promptly detained by Border Patrol agents, she says, adding that agents often park their SUVs at the edge of the golf course.

River Bend Resort is owned by John Allburg, who incorporated the business in 1983 as River Bend Resort, Inc. Allburg refused to comment for this article. A scan of the Federal Election Commission and Texas Ethics Commission databases did not find any political contributions linked to Allburg.

The Border Fence Affects Only Poor Residents

Just 69 miles north, Daniel Garza, 76, faces a similar situation with a neighbor who has political connections that reach the

White House. In the small town of Granjeno, population 313, Garza points to a field across the street where a segment of the proposed 18-foot high border wall would abruptly end after passing through his brick home and a small, yellow house he gave his son. "All that land over there is owned by the Hunts," he says, waving a hand toward the horizon. "The wall doesn't go there."

In this area everyone knows the Hunts. Dallas billionaire Ray L. Hunt and his relatives are one of the wealthiest oil and gas dynasties in the world. Hunt, a close friend of President George W. Bush, recently donated $35 million to Southern Methodist University to help build Bush's presidential library. In 2001, Bush made him a member of the Foreign Intelligence Advisory Board, where Hunt received a security clearance and access to classified intelligence.

Over the years, Hunt has transformed his 6,000-acre property, called the Sharyland Plantation, from acres of onions and vegetables into swathes of exclusive, gated communities where houses sell from $650,000 to $1 million and residents enjoy golf courses, elementary schools, and a sports park. The plantation contains a 1,800-acre business park and Sharyland Utilities, run by Hunt's son Hunter, which delivers electricity to plantation residents and Mexican factories.

The development's Web site touts its proximity to the international border and the new Anzalduas International Bridge now under construction, built on land Hunt donated. Hunt has also formed Hunt Mexico with a wealthy Mexican business partner to develop both sides of the border into a lucrative trade corridor the size of Manhattan.

Jeanne Phillips, a spokesperson for Hunt Consolidated, Inc., says that since the company is private, it doesn't have to identify the Mexican partner. Phillips says, however, that no one from the company has been directly involved in siting the fence. "We, like other citizens in the Valley, have waited for the federal government to designate the location of the wall," she says.

Garza stands in front of his modest brick home, which he built for his retirement after 50 years as a migrant farm worker. For the past five months, he has stayed awake nights trying to find a way to stop the gears of bureaucracy from grinding over his home.

Most border residents couldn't believe the fence would ever be built through their homes and communities. They expected it to run along the banks of the Rio Grande.

A February 8 [2008] announcement by Homeland Security Secretary Michael Chertoff said the agency would settle for building the fence atop the levee behind Garza's house instead of through it, which has given Garza some hope. Like Tamez, he wonders why his home and small town were targeted by Homeland Security in the first place.

"I don't see why they have to destroy my home, my land, and let the wall end there." He points across the street to Hunt's land. "How will that stop illegal immigration?"

Building a Border Fence Has More to Do with Politics than with Stopping Illegal Immigrants

Most border residents couldn't believe the fence would ever be built through their homes and communities. They expected it to run along the banks of the Rio Grande, not north of the flood levees—in some cases like Tamez's, as far as a mile north of the river. So it came as a shock last summer when residents were approached by uniformed Border Patrol agents. They asked people to sign waivers allowing Homeland Security to survey their properties for construction of the wall. When they declined, Homeland Security filed condemnation suits.

In time, local landowners realized that the fence's location had everything to do with politics and private profit, and nothing to do with stopping illegal immigration.

In 2006, Congress passed the Secure Fence Act, authored by Republican Congressman Peter King from New York. The legislation mandated that 700 miles of double-fencing be built along the southern border from California to Texas. The bill detailed where the fencing, or, as many people along the border call it, "the wall," would be built. After a year of inflamed rhetoric about the plague of illegal immigration and Congress's failure to pass comprehensive immigration reform, the bill passed with overwhelming support from Republicans and a few Democrats. All the Texas border members of the U.S. House of Representatives, except San Antonio Republican Henry Bonilla, voted against it. Texas Sens. Kay Bailey Hutchison and John Cornyn voted for the bill.

On August 10, 2007, Chertoff announced his agency would scale back the initial 700 miles of fencing to 370 miles, to be built in segments across the southern border. Chertoff cited budget shortages and technological difficulties as justifications for not complying with the bill.

How did his agency decide where to build the segments? Chad Foster, the mayor of Eagle Pass, says he thought it was a simple enough question and that the answer would be based on data and facts. Foster chairs the Texas Border Coalition. TBC, as Foster calls it, is a group of border mayors and business leaders who have repeatedly traveled to Washington [D.C.] for the past 18 months to try to get federal officials to listen to them.

Foster says he has never received any logical answers from Homeland Security as to why certain areas in his city had been targeted for fencing over other areas. "I puzzled a while over why the fence would bypass the industrial park and go through the city park," he says.

Despite terse meetings with Chertoff, Foster and other coalition members say the conversation has been one-sided.

"I think we have a government within a government," Foster says. "[This is] a tremendous bureaucracy—DHS is just a monster."

The [*Texas*] *Observer* called Homeland Security in Washington to find out how it had decided where to build the fence. The voice mail system sputtered through a dizzying array of acronyms: DOJ, USACE, CBP, and USCIS. On the second call a media spokesperson with a weary voice directed queries to Michael Friel, the fence spokesman for Customs and Border Protection. Six calls and two e-mails later, Friel responded with a curt e-mail: "Got your message. Working on answers . . ." it said. Days passed, and Friel's answers never came.

Seeking Congressional Response

Since Homeland Security wasn't providing answers, perhaps Congress would. Phone conversations with congressional offices ranged from "but they aren't even building a wall" to "I don't know. That's a good question." At the sixth congressional office contacted, a GOP [Grand Old Party Republican] staffer who asked not to be identified, but who is familiar with the fence, says the fencing locations stemmed from statistics showing high apprehension and narcotic seizure rates. This seems questionable, since maps released by the U.S. Army Corps of Engineers showed the wall going through such properties as the University of Texas at Brownsville—hardly a hotbed for drug smugglers and immigrant trafficking.

Questioned more about where the data came from, the staffer said she would enquire further. The next day she called back. "The border fence is being handled by Greg Giddens at the Secure Border Initiative Office [SBI] within the U.S. Customs and Border Protection office," she said.

Giddens is executive director of the SBI, as it is called, which is in charge of SBInet, a consortium of private contractors led by Boeing Co. The group received a multibillion dollar contract in 2006 to secure the northern and southern borders with a network of vehicle barriers, fencing, and surveillance systems. Companies Boeing chose to secure the southern border from terrorists include DRS Technologies Inc., Kollsman Inc., L-3 Communications Inc., Perot Systems Corp., and a unit of Unisys Corp.

A February 2007 audit by the U.S. Government Accountability Office [GAO] cited Homeland Security and the SBInet project for poor fiscal oversight and a lack of demonstrable objectives. The GAO audit team recommended that Homeland Security place a spending limit on the Boeing contract for SBInet since the company had been awarded an "indefinite delivery/indefinite quantity contract for 3 years with three 1-year options."

The agency rejected the auditors' recommendation, saying 6,000 miles of border is limitation enough.

Outsourcing the Border Fence

In a February 2007 hearing, Congressman Henry Waxman, a California Democrat and the chairman of the [House] Oversight and Government Reform Committee, had more scathing remarks for Giddens and the SBInet project. "As of December [2007], the Department of Homeland Security had hired a staff of 98 to oversee the new SBInet contract. This may seem like progress until you ask who these overseers are. More than half are private contractors. Some of these private contractors even work for companies that are business partners of Boeing, the company they are supposed to be overseeing. And from what we are now learning from the department, this may be just the tip of the iceberg."

Waxman said of SBInet that "virtually every detail is being outsourced from the government to private contractors. The government is relying on private contractors to design the programs, build them, and even conduct oversight over them."

A phone call to Giddens at SBI is referred to Loren Flossman, who's in charge of tactical infrastructure for the office. Flossman says all data regarding the placement of the fence [are] classified because "you don't want to tell the very people you're trying to keep from coming across the methodology used to deter them."

Flossman also calls the University of Texas [UT] at Brownsville campus a problem area for illegal immigration. "I wouldn't assume that these are folks that aren't intelligent enough that if they dress a certain way, they're gonna fit in," he says.

Chief John Cardoza, head of the UT-Brownsville police, says the Border Patrol would have to advise his police force of any immigrant smuggling or narcotic seizures that happen on campus. "If it's happening on my campus, I'm not being told about it," he says. Cardoza says he has never come across illegal immigrants dressed as students.

Flossman goes on to say that Boeing isn't building the fence, but is providing steel for it. Eric Mazzacone, a spokesman for Boeing, refers the *Observer* to Michael Friel at Customs and Border Protection, and intercedes to get him on the phone. Friel confirms that Boeing has just finished building a 30-mile stretch of fence in Arizona, but insists other questions be submitted in writing.

The Politics of Building a Fence

Boeing, a multibillion dollar aero-defense company, is the second-largest defense contractor in the nation. The company has powerful board members, such as William M. Daley, former U.S. secretary of commerce; retired General James L. Jones, former supreme allied commander in Europe; and Kenneth M. Duberstein, a former White House chief of staff. The corporation is also one of the biggest political contributors in Washington, giving more than $9 million to Democratic and Republican members of Congress in the last decade. In 2006, the year the Secure Fence Act was passed, Boeing gave more than $1.4 million to Democrats and Republicans, according to the Center for Responsive Politics.

A majority of this money has gone to legislators such as Congressman Duncan Hunter, the California Republican who championed the Secure Fence Act. In 2006, Hunter received at least $10,000 from Boeing and more than $93,000 from defense companies bidding for the SBInet contract, according to the center. During his failed bid this year for the White House, Hunter made illegal immigration and building a border fence the major themes of his campaign.

Boeing continues to hire companies for the SBInet project. And the congressional districts of backers of the border fence continue to benefit.

In early February 2008, Chertoff asked Congress for $12 billion for border security. He included $775 million for the SBInet program, despite the fact that congressional leaders still can't get straight answers from Homeland Security about the program. As recently as January 31 [2008], Senate Homeland Security and Governmental Affairs Committee members sent a letter to Chertoff asking for "greater clarity on [the Customs and Border Protection office's] operational objectives for SBInet and the projected milestones and anticipated costs for the project." They have yet to receive a response.

Boeing continues to hire companies for the SBInet project. And the congressional districts of backers of the border fence continue to benefit. A recent *Long Island [New York] Business News* article trumpeted the success of Telephonics Corp., a local business, in Congressman King's congressional district that won a $14.5 million bid to provide a mobile surveillance system under SBInet to protect the southern border.

While Garza and Tamez wait for answers, they say they are being asked to sacrifice something that can't be replaced by money. They are giving up their land, their homes, their heritage, and the few remaining acres left to them that they hoped to pass on to their children and grandchildren.

"I am an old man. I have colon cancer, and I am 76 years old," Garza says, resting against a tree in front of his home. "All I do is worry about whether they will take my home. My wife keeps asking me, 'What are we going to do?'"

Besides these personal tragedies, Eagle Pass Mayor Foster says there is another tragedy in store for the American taxpayer. A 2006 congressional report estimates the cost of maintaining and building the fence could be as much as $49 billion over its expected 25-year life span.

"They are just going to push this problem on the next administration, and nobody is going to talk about immigration reform, and that's the illness," Foster says. "The wall is a Band-Aid on the problem. And to blow $49 billion and not walk away with a secure border—that's a travesty."

12

The Minutemen Have Helped Secure the Border

Glynn Custred

Glynn Custred is a professor of anthropology at California State University, East Bay (formerly Hayward), and is on the board of directors for the California Association of Scholars.

Government response to the wave of illegal immigrants crossing the U.S. border with Mexico has been lackluster. Politics is keeping the Border Patrol from expanding its operations and choking off major paths of entry. In Arizona, outraged citizens who are tired of their government's inactivity have established the Minuteman Project to patrol these arteries into the country and report illegal entry to border authorities. The Minutemen have been very successful in thwarting the influx of illegals in Arizona, despite receiving no aid or recognition from Washington, D.C. Residents in Minutemen-patrolled regions, however, are thankful that this organization has taken action and made this part of the nation safer and more secure.

In eastern and central Arizona the border between the United States and Mexico runs in a straight surveyor's line through mile after mile of scrubland. It is a vast and empty terrain punctuated by barren mountains that rise sharply above the desert. The international line is marked only by 19th-century obelisks of concrete or iron, standing just a few feet high in the desert brush, spaced at intervals of 0.14 to 4.91 miles. The

Glynn Custred, "Where Are My Juice and Crackers?" *American Spectator*, vol. 38, July/August 2005, pp. 20–25.

only indication of the border between the markers is a fence strung by ranchers to keep cattle from straying and a rough dirt road that runs beside it.

By day the countryside is quiet. Dust devils occasionally swirl upward and spin furiously across the creosote plain, and tumble weeds lifted by sudden gusts of wind sometimes sail over the border fence and bounce on the dirt road before bumping into the cactus and desert brush on the other side.

But when the sun sets, the quiet landscape comes alive. Groups of migrants emerge from the mesquite and the arroyos where they have hidden all day to avoid detection from aircraft. They put on their backpacks and pick up their water bottles, then head north. Many walk only as far as prearranged points along a country road where smugglers pick them up, sometimes in stolen or hijacked vehicles, then race at high speeds in the dark with their lights off.

Many others walk for miles into the interior where they can continue in comfort to their final destination, which may be anywhere within the United States, for once beyond the border American authorities have no further interest in them. All along the way on the U.S. side of the border one sees trash of all kinds littering the route of this vast migration.

Dave Stoddard lives just north of the border near the San Pedro River, the route the Spanish explorer Coronado used in 1540 when he entered what would 308 years later become a part of the United States. Today it is one of the many routes of mass migration northward.

Stoddard says that Americans living near the border and those who live in the interior along the favorite routes of migration complain of a constant crowd hurrying past their homes all night long, especially between 1:00 and 3:00 in the morning. Residents have put locks on their houses, their barns, and their out-buildings. They have built fences and installed motion sensor lights, and have posted guard dogs that bark all night long in order to gain a sense of uneasy security. For with a massive uncontrolled migration passing by your back door night after night you never know who will come to rob and assault you, especially since desperate men transporting drugs sometimes travel with the passing migrants.

Husbands and wives cannot go out for an evening together unless they have someone to watch the house while they're gone, and since the distances are great in the borderlands—the minimum time of response for a 911 call to the sheriff is around 30 minutes—everyone is armed. Men wear sidearms at work and mothers put handguns in their purses when they walk their children to the school bus. The elderly say they feel like prisoners in their own homes.

The Minuteman Project Halts Migration

Then on the first of April 2005 the migration came to a sudden halt. From the town of Douglas to the tiny settlement of Naco, and from there all the way to the other side of the San Pedro River some 40 miles to the west, the nocturnal movement ceased. Dogs no longer barked all night long, and people said they had not slept so well in years.

Though poll after poll reveals that the public wants the government to bring illegal immigration under control, the President [George W. Bush] is content to keep things just the way they are.

The reason: the presence of a small group of civilian volunteers called the Minutemen who mounted a month-long vigil to demonstrate that, with proper vigilance, the stream of illegal migration could indeed be stopped. The project, organized by Chris Simcox of Tombstone, Arizona, and James Gilchrist of southern California, was based on the neighborhood watch model, a civilian association whose function, according to the Neighborhood Watch Institute, is to provide "eyes and ears for law enforcement."

If any law enforcement agency needs this kind of help it is the United States Border Patrol. Since March 2003 the Border Patrol has been a part of the Department of Homeland Security with the revised mission of preventing terrorists and terrorist material from crossing the border—this on top of its already demanding mission of interdicting drug smuggling and the control of illegal immigration, tasks made all but impossible by the massive stream of illegal migration pouring across the border.

Border Patrol union president T.J. Bonner, of the National Border Patrol Council, rightly observes: "Even if a terrorist is one-in-a-million occurrence, with several million people coming into the country each year, very soon they reach that critical mass necessary to carry out another attack on the magnitude of September 11 [2001 terrorist attacks (9/11)]. This is totally unacceptable from the standpoint of homeland security and national security. We should gain control of our borders."

[Mexican] soldiers interdicted would-be border crossers, loaded them into trucks, and transported them to points along the border where they could cross illegally into the United States beyond the eyes and ears of the Minutemen.

Minutemen Do Not Have Government Support

After 9/11, George [W.] Bush called for public participation in homeland security. Yet when asked about the Minuteman Project, President Bush bristled, calling the volunteers "vigilantes." Though poll after poll reveals that the public wants the government to bring illegal immigration under control, the President is content to keep things just the way they are since it creates the *de facto* amnesty he has promised Mexican president Vicente Fox and that he has been unable to pass through Congress.

The "eyes and ears" of citizens on the border is the last thing Bush and the Mexican government want. The Mexican elite regard the massive exodus from Mexico as a safety-valve that protects their own privileged position; as a cash cow for Mexico in the form of remittances to the tune of $14 billion each year, the second largest source of income for Mexico after oil; and as a potential means for manipulating the American political system (as frankly revealed by such Mexican leaders as former President Ernesto Zedillo and former national security advisor and later U.N. [United Nations] ambassador Adolfo Aquilar Zinser).

In order to avoid unwanted publicity, the Border Patrol assigned 500 more agents for quick response to reports from Minutemen of illegal movement. The Mexican government likewise dispatched police, as well as Mexican army troops, by one estimate 1,600 strong, to their side of the border to dampen potentially damaging publicity because of the presence of observers on the American side of the line. Soldiers interdicted would-be border crossers, loaded them into trucks, and transported them to points along the border where they could cross illegally into the United States beyond the eyes and ears of the Minutemen.

Illegal aliens are some of the most violent criminals in the United States today.

The Public Outrage over Illegal Immigration

Americans are becoming increasingly resentful of the government's refusal to do anything about illegal immigration. Americans do not resent the migrants themselves. On the whole Americans regard them as industrious, good-hearted people looking for a way to better their lives and those of their family by hard work. Many Americans, especially those who live along the border, admire their perseverance, saying that in their place they would do the same.

But breaking the law is not the best way to start a new life in a country that claims to be based on the rule of law. There is also a darker undercurrent within the uncontrolled stream of illegal immigrants—the influx of hardened criminals who come to commit crime. "As long as our borders remain porous, they are just as open to criminals and terrorists as they are to illegal aliens," says T.J. Bonner.

Illegal aliens are some of the most violent criminals in the United States today. In an article in the *[New York] City Journal*, Heather MacDonald reports that illegal aliens account for 95 percent of all outstanding warrants for homicide (out of a total of 1,200 to 1,500). This figure is up by two-thirds for all felony warrants (17,000). Illegal immigration also feeds the growing membership of violent gangs.

The public is also becoming increasingly aware of the cost to taxpayers of supporting high levels of illegal immigration. Harvard economist George Borjas, in his book *Heaven's Door*, says that today's immigrants, of which a major percentage are illegal, possess fewer skills and are more dependent on public assistance than their predecessors, and that their children, unlike the children of previous waves of immigrants, are less likely to follow the upwardly mobile tract. He writes that they are more likely to remain poor and live in segregated communities.

Moreover, he says, the inexhaustible influx of cheap, exploitable labor adds little to the overall economy. He calculates that the net annual gain, as of 1999, was only about $8 billion per year. Yet by dragging down wages for those native born at the lower end of the economic scale, Borjas estimates that some $160 million per year is shifted away from workers and toward employers and consumers of public services.

Taxes paid by immigrants as a group are low due to their disproportionately low-skill status and thus their low level of income, while their consumption of tax-supported services are high due to their high fertility and poverty rates, factors made far more significant by the large proportion of illegal immigrants among them.

The Cost of Illegal Immigration

Recently the National Research Council estimated that the total cost to the taxpayer of illegal immigration, which is carried mainly by local and state governments, is $11 to $22 billion a year for education, criminal justice, and medical care. Once a child is born to illegal aliens, the child is eligible for welfare since people born in the United States are American citizens. Illegal residents who have such "anchor babies" can tap into the welfare system, thus adding to the total bill the taxpayer picks up for illegal immigration. California alone has a net cost of $3 billion dollars in a single year for such services.

Uncontrolled illegal immigration is pushing down wages at the lower end of the income scale, incurring high costs to the taxpayer, and depriving the government of revenue it needs to meet its obligations.

The problem is most critical for hospitals. By law anyone coming to an emergency room must be treated. Since illegal workers are not covered by insurance, they use emergency room service as their sole source of health care. The cost falls to the hospital, whether private or public, to the point where some facilities have simply closed their doors. When the federal government proposed to spend $4 billion partially to reimburse doctors and hospitals, many native-born working poor asked why they should be burdened with debt to pay medical bills while their taxes subsidize the free care of people who are in the country illegally.

Remittances each year also remove billions of dollars from circulation within the American economy, and the underground economy created by illegal immigration is, according to some economists, growing at perhaps a faster rate than the legitimate economy, thus costing the federal government hundreds of billions of dollars in lost taxes, money that if collected would wipe out the current budget deficit. The exploitation of cheap immigrant labor is therefore by no means cheap for taxpayers who are in essence subsidizing many special interest groups that profit from cheap foreign labor.

Uncontrolled illegal immigration is pushing down wages at the lower end of the income scale, incurring high costs to the taxpayer, and depriving the government of revenue it needs to meet its obligations. That the second generation of immigrants will not assimilate in the way other waves of immigrants eventually did poses another troubling problem. Sociologists Alejandro Portes and Ruben Rimbaut, in *Legacies: The Story of the Immigrant Second Generation*, say that the "transformative potential, for better or for worse," of the second generation "is immense" with the possibility that it will "catalyze a quantum leap in social problems." In a similar vein Harvard scholar and political scientist Samuel P. Huntington, warns in his latest book *Who Are We?* that "nothing less than our national identity is at stake" if the historically unprecedented wave of mass migration is allowed to continue.

Government Inaction

Despite the downside of massive sustained illegal immigration, the government has systematically abandoned the enforcement of the nation's immigration laws. This began under President [Bill] Clinton when he stopped enforcing employer sanctions, penalties for employers who knowingly hire illegal aliens, and by reducing border management to nothing more than an expensive, dishonest, and demoralizing display of empty ritual.

The Clinton administration did not act alone. Some members of the very Congress that passed the laws in the first place pressured enforcement agencies not to enforce the law at the behest of business interests that profit from an unchecked flow of tractable labor. The [George W.] Bush administration completed the process by ending what remained of interior enforcement and by continuing the charade of border controls.

The Livermore Sector of the Border Patrol in the San Francisco Bay Area was, according to one former senior Border Patrol official, "man for man the most productive in the country." It was shut down in 2004.

The 9/11 Commission recommended an increase in the manpower of the Border Patrol, and in 2005, following those recommendations Congress authorized the hiring of 2,000 more Border Patrol agents. But the president's budget allocated only enough money for 210 agents, not even enough to cover attrition. When asked about the paltry sum, outgoing Homeland Security chief Tom Ridge said that money for such purposes is "fool's gold."

[Illegal immigrants] know that once across the line they are home free, and that if caught at the border they will be returned to try again until they make it.

Since June 2004 the Border Patrol has been restricted to the border itself and to stationary points, thus ending one of its traditional missions—sweeping interior regions for illegal aliens. One frustrated agent says this unprecedented policy is the equivalent of putting a ten-yard limit on bank robbery: if the robber gets beyond that point he can keep the money.

Joe Dessaro, a recently retired Border Patrol agent and union chief, wrote in his farewell letter to the union that the Border Patrol is "one of the most inefficient and misleading agencies in the history of government." Echoing this sentiment another agent hundreds of miles away observes that "the whole thing is the biggest bunco job in history, spending millions not to do the job."

None of this is lost on those who would cross the border illegally. They know that once across the line they are home free, and that if caught at the border they will be returned to try again until they make it. One agent says he caught the same man three times in one shift at the same place on the fence. Border crossers also know the routine. When they are picked up and put in vans, some ask, "Where are my juice and crackers?"

Growing Public Frustration

Special interests and a growing illegal immigration lobby have been able to completely trump majority opinion on immigration, leaving the public little opportunity to express its wishes. One means employed by the public to get around special interest obstruction is the ballot initiative.

The Minuteman Project was yet another attempt by frustrated and increasingly angry citizens to express their opposition to a de facto open-border policy.

In 1992 when the flow of illegal entrants created such havoc on the border and became such an obvious drain on public services, the people of California passed, by a margin of 59 percent, Proposition 187, a ballot measure designed to deny public benefits to anyone in the country illegally. A federal judge and later a Democratic governor, both using questionable means, showed contempt both for the people's will and the democratic process when they jettisoned the new law.

In 2005 frustrated citizens tried another ballot initiative, Proposition 200 in Arizona, but given the kind of obstruction we know so well it will probably never be enforced.

The Minuteman Project was yet another attempt by frustrated and increasingly angry citizens to express their opposition to a de facto open-border policy. The project worked.

During the next to the last week of the vigil, Richard Humphries, a Minuteman coordinator and local resident, took me in his jeep along the border between Naco and the San Pedro River. As we traveled the rutted road we saw no signs of illegal entry along what had been just three weeks before a major route of illegal entry. The countryside was deserted except for a rancher driving his pick-up truck on the other side of the rickety border fence, and a lone man casually walking towards a corral near the San Pedro River which is used as a staging ground for illegal crossings.

"Que tal! A donde va?" we asked (meaning: "Hi! Where are you going")? With a broad grin he said in English, "The United States." If that is what he had in mind he was one of the very few that month, at least along that stretch of the line.

When asked how things were going, a Border Patrolman on duty smiled and said suggestively, "Quiet." We chatted with another on-duty agent for a few minutes. As we were leaving he called out, "I'm not supposed to say this, but you guys are doing a great job!" and then gave a big thumbs-up.

The Minutemen Are Effective

The Border Patrol management seems to have thought that the Minutemen had done an effective job, because after the project had ended and the volunteers had gone home, agents at Naco were told not to arrest illegal aliens in their section for fear that a jump in the apprehension rate would confirm the project's success.

Critics say the project did nothing more than push the stream of migration around the manned observation posts. Minutemen, however, said that their presence proved that border controls could work if serious vigils were mounted similar to the one they operated during the month of April. Since the formal democratic process remains closed to the majority of the public on this issue, it will take more such demonstrations before the political elites become responsive to a major policy issue that involves such serious consequences both for the short and the long term.

Chris Simcox promises more border watches along both the Mexican and the Canadian borders. And a border watch is planned for California in August or earlier, apparently with the approval of Governor Arnold Schwarzenegger.

This much is certain: People along the border where the Minutemen held their watch appreciated the peaceful month it gave them. In a half-page ad in the Sunday *Sierra Vista [Arizona] Herald* local residents told them: "Thanks for doing what our government won't . . . close the border to illegal aliens. It was the quietest month we've had in many years . . . you made us feel safe."

13

The Minutemen Have Not Helped to Secure the Border

David Neiwert

David Neiwert is a journalist based in Seattle. He received the National Press Club Award for Distinguished Online Journalism and is the author of several books, including his most recent, The Eliminationists: How Hate Talk Radicalized the American Right.

The Minuteman Civil Defense Corps, which began in 2003, was meant to be a civilian-run watchdog organization that would help deter illegal immigrant crossings along the Arizona border. While it initially earned praise for its grassroots response to a national concern, infighting has diminished the effectiveness of the Minutemen's efforts. Money raised for building fences disappeared, white supremacists infiltrated the ranks, and a rift between two major figures revealed that the movement was not united in its strategy. Declining membership and a lack of funds eventually sapped the group's strength, reducing its success in securing the border between the United States and Mexico.

Jim Campbell was a contractor before he became an Arizona retiree, so he happens to know a little about getting construction projects completed. He also happens to be avidly involved in efforts to stem what he and thousands of others see as an unholy tide of illegal immigrants streaming over the

David Neiwert, "The Fence to Nowhere," *American Prospect*, vol. 19, September 22, 2008, pp. 16–19.

U.S.–Mexico border. So when the Minutemen—those "citizen watchdogs" who have been setting up vigilante border patrols throughout the Southwest—announced plans to build a fence along a section of the Arizona–Mexico border, it seemed to Campbell like a good time to step up and make a difference.

A couple of years later and $100,000 lighter, Campbell's not so sure it was a good idea. In fact, he calls the people running the Minutemen's border-fence project "a bunch of felons."

When he first contacted the Minuteman Civil Defense Corps (MCDC)—the most prominent of the two major Minutemen organizations and the sponsors of the fence project—in early May 2006, he was enthusiastic about his vision: "miles and miles of steel!" Campbell offered to donate $100,000 immediately so the Minutemen could buy steel posts—the first step in building an "Israeli style" security fence—and install them in time for the groundbreaking ceremony. He took out a loan on his home and wired the money to the MCDC's parent organization, the Washington, D.C.-based Declaration Alliance. Campbell was told his was the largest single donation out of the thousands that were pouring in for the fence project.

Welcome to the world of the Minutemen, where all-American values provide a nice storefront for a financial black hole that vacuums up hundreds of thousands of donors' dollars.

But when Campbell attended the MCDC's big groundbreaking event a few weeks later, the five-strand barbed-wire fence being erected by volunteers was a far cry from what he thought he had funded. After a flurry of negotiations with the MCDC's president, Chris Simcox, Campbell agreed to spend another $63,000 of his own money on steel posts for a "serious" fence at another site—believing the MCDC would later repay him.

A year later, with nothing more to show for his money either in fence construction or reimbursement, he filed a lawsuit for $1.2 million seeking reimbursement and damages. In a letter to his lawyer, he observes that his donation "will have been squandered in a seemingly well-intentioned but short-lived 'monument to deceit' on the border. It is clear to me now that this fence project was conceived as a grand facade—a scheme—to attract endless streams of donations from the public who placed blind faith (as I did) in both the sincerity and trustworthiness of its promoters."

Like nearly every right-wing populist movement from which the Minutemen are descended, they have crumbled under the weight of financial mismanagement, competing egos, and political infighting.

Welcome to the world of the Minutemen, where all-American values provide a nice storefront for a financial black hole that vacuums up hundreds of thousands of donors' dollars. The group fits into a long tradition of right-wing political organizing that runs from the resurrected Ku Klux Klan of the 1920s to the tax-protest movement of the 1980s and the militias of the 1990s. In the end, these efforts are mostly scams: They serve up a heady concoction of jingoistic fervor, bigoted xenophobia, and paranoid conspiracy theories as a means to salve all that ails the patriotic soul—but largely they have the mysterious effect of separating their fellow right-wingers from their money. And as these groups dissolve into scandal and infighting, they leave far more radical splinter groups in their wake.

The History of the Minutemen

To understand the Minutemen, it helps to consider their origins: They are, after all, essentially a militia. When Chris Simcox began organizing civilian border-watch patrols in early

2003 in his hometown of Tombstone, Arizona, he called his outfit the Tombstone Militia, eventually changed to the Civil Homeland Defense Corps. Simcox incorporated "Minuteman" into the name of his operation in 2005 when he hooked up with a California ex-Marine named Jim Gilchrist, who had founded a similar group he called the Minuteman Project. Both groups have consistently identified with the "militia" (or "patriot") movement, which in the 1990s revolved around hysterical fears that a cadre of government conspirators intended to start rounding up gun owners and other citizens and placing them in concentration camps. The Minutemen blend this conspiracy theory with their own special brand of xenophobia—notably, the claim that Latino immigrants are part of a grand "reconquista" plot by Mexico to reclaim the Southwestern United States. And, like nearly every right-wing populist movement from which the Minutemen are descended, they have crumbled under the weight of financial mismanagement, competing egos, and political infighting.

The Simcox-Gilchrist partnership produced a national sensation in April 2005, when dozens of volunteers took part in the Minutemen's month-long border-watch operation. At times, journalists and camera crews outnumbered the actual watchers; it made great prime-time content for FOX News and CNN's resident anti-immigrant talking head, Lou Dobbs. Simcox and Gilchrist were the faces of the movement, and they appeared on air so frequently that they practically became household names.

Their synergy, however, was short-lived. That fall, Gilchrist and Simcox had discussed handing over the Minutemen's financial and public-relations operations to a conservative Beltway organization called Diener Consultants and an associated outfit called the Declaration Alliance, run by onetime Republican presidential candidate Alan Keyes. Both groups had been consultants in Gilchrist's failed congressional bid earlier that year, and Gilchrist later told his board members that the Diener Consultants and Keyes's organization "stole my money." He wanted nothing further to do with them. Simcox, on the other hand, wanted to continue.

A Rift in the Group

So in December 2005, they went their separate ways, and the Minutemen officially became two organizations. They had overlapping missions, but each chose different strategies: Gilchrist's focus was going to be on border watches, while Simcox's MCDC was to be a national anti-immigration enterprise that would build chapters in all 50 states. In the end, the two groups followed remarkably similar paths into dysfunction.

Of the promised 70 miles of security fence, so far a length of only .7 miles has been erected.

That spring and summer [2006], Gilchrist was primarily occupied with self-promotion. He went on a cross-country tour to promote his book [Minutemen: The Battle to Secure America's Borders] and met with Constitution Party officials about the possibility of a presidential bid (nothing came of the talk). Meanwhile, Simcox's MCDC organized a follow-up border watch in Arizona in April 2006, and the group began recruiting new Minutemen around the country—everywhere from Illinois to Washington to New Hampshire. The donations began pouring in. Now thoroughly enmeshed in the Keyes organization, all the MCDC donations flowed into a web of nearly a dozen organizations revolving around Declaration Alliance, including Diener Consultants; a Texas outfit called American Caging that acted as the escrow agent and comptroller for the operation; Renew America, a Keyes-run "grassroots organization"; and a direct-mail company called Response Unlimited.

The association with Keyes' organizations raised hackles within MCDC ranks. Some of the Minutemen began exchanging e-mails denouncing the relationships, since Keyes and his groups were perceived within the ultra-right ranks as being "neoconservative" organizations whose interests were inimical to theirs. Gilchrist, who had washed his hands of the Keyes groups, sent out a bulletin making clear that his Minuteman Project no longer had any associations with Simcox and his outfit. The *Washington [D.C.] Times* reported on the dissent and quoted Keyes dismissing the MCDC's internal critics as anti-immigrant racists "and other unsavory fringe elements attempting to hijack the border security debate to further their individual agendas."

Simcox was undeterred. In April 2006, he hit on the idea of building a "state of the art" security fence along a section of the Arizona–Mexico border and told the *Washington Times* that he had more than $200,000 in donations. He described the project as one that would "feature separate, 14-foot-high fences on both sides of the border, separated by a roadway to allow the passage of U.S. Border Patrol vehicles, with surveillance cameras and motion sensors." It was this description that enticed Jim Campbell to pony up his $100,000. But there were problems, notably that there were few private landholders along the border willing to participate. The ranch owner who had agreed to a fence had no interest in an "Israeli style" security barrier; he only wanted a standard barbed-wire fence to keep out Mexican cattle. So that was what was built. The steel Campbell bought was to be used for a short section of "demonstration" fence at another ranch. Of the promised 70 miles of security fence, so far a length of only .7 miles has been erected. Much of Campbell's steel still lies in a pile, collecting Arizona dust.

The Funding for the Fence Disappears

Jim Campbell wasn't the only one making things difficult for Simcox. In May 2007, a group of state-level organizers held a meeting to air their grievances over the way Simcox was running the operation: promised funds never delivered, the heavy-handed leadership style, and the general lack of accountability. In particular, they wanted to know what had become of the $1.6 million that Simcox had told the press the organization had brought in, since they were seeing precious little of it spent at the state level.

Simcox abruptly fired them all the next week. The dissenters, led by Simcox's former Arizona chapter head, Stacey O'Connell, regrouped and within a couple of months had formed a rival organization calling itself the Patriots Border Alliance. O'Connell continues to openly criticize the MCDC over its murky finances, appearing on radio talk shows and circulating what information he can glean about the MCDC's money. "I joined an organization that I thought stood for the rule of law and was transparent and was part of the American spirit," O'Connell says. "And to watch what has happened over the past couple of years has really faltered the ideas of the movement."

Certainly there was a significant gap between Simcox's public claims of having raised $1.6 million for the fence, and what his financial disclosure forms show his organization actually spent on it. No one can say for sure because the MCDC won't let anyone touch its books. But a look at the organization's 2006 public filings indicates that, of all the money raised for the border fence, only a small amount (if any at all) went toward its construction. The forms for the Declaration Alliance—through whom all the border-fence donations were directed—show that it brought in nearly $5 million that year for all its programs. What percentage of that $5 million consisted of border-fence donations is unclear, but considering that the fence appeals began in May 2006 and have remained the MCDC's (and Declaration Alliance's) chief fundraising focus in the months since, it is likely that they provided at least a majority of that money. It also shows that

$3.19 million went to the MCDC. But for what? The Declaration Alliance largely spent the money on printing, consulting, and similar activities. The only indication on the form that any actual money went back to the MCDC in the field is $143,000 listed as "operational expenses," though this money reportedly was for MCDC border watches, not the fence project. If any of those millions of dollars actually went toward building a border fence, it's difficult to ascertain where they are and how much was disbursed—though a look at the disclosure form for the Minuteman Foundation, the MCDC entity set up specifically to handle the fence project, shows a mere $87,500 in total revenues from donations for 2006. If that's the actual revenue coming from that $3.19 million the Declaration Alliance says it spent on the MCDC—and you estimate that at least half of that is fence-related—then we're talking about less than 6 percent coming back to build the fence.

In other words, the best rough estimate is that about 94 cents of every dollar Jim Campbell spent on the fence went toward printing, mailing, consulting, and the like. It's no wonder members at the field level were seeing so little of the money that Simcox claimed to be rolling in.

Without offering specifics, Simcox denies what the financial-disclosure forms show. "I know there's a lot of controversy over the funding," he says. "But it's just absurd. Every penny that we raised went into the surveying, the engineering, and the construction of what we could build with what we brought in. It's difficult to complete a project when you don't have the funding."

Donors Want to Recover Their Money

While Simcox faltered under the weight of his members' demands for transparency, his former cohort Gilchrist found his Minuteman Project [MMP] embroiled in a strikingly similar controversy. The problem began in November 2006, when Gilchrist began bouncing checks. The MMP's board of directors grew concerned and began asking to see bank statements, as well as a copy of the organization's bylaws. Gilchrist promised but never delivered any of the requested documents. The more the board members looked into the way Gilchrist was handling the MMP's finances, the more alarmed they became.

The issue came to a head in a series of board meetings in December, when board members raised the possibility that funds had been embezzled. Gilchrist accused the board of acting like a "lynch mob" and demanded they cease their inquiry. The wrangling continued over the next few weeks until the board voted to terminate Gilchrist as the MMP president and to dismiss two of his lieutenants for fiduciary misdeeds. Three days later, Gilchrist showed up at a board meeting at the MMP offices and announced, "You are all fired! You are all fired!" There was another meeting on February 2, which turned so confrontational that sheriff's deputies were called.

Today the minuteman movement is beyond mere disarray; it is in the early stages of complete decay.

Since then, the matter has devolved into a blizzard of lawsuits, with each side suing the other and variously claiming victory as the rulings and dismissals pile up. At last count, the MMP board had refiled its lawsuit for fraud, and Gilchrist was pursuing individual suits against its members. When he talks about the case now, Gilchrist comes across as rather paranoid. He told me he believes the board members have an ulterior motive: "And that is to jam the Minuteman movement—not just my project but the entire movement across the country."

For their part, the MMP board members insist this is about financial accountability. "If we were mean and vicious and dumb, we would want Gilchrist in jail," says Paul Sielski, board member Deborah Courtney's husband and one of the plaintiffs. "But at the end of the day, we don't want him to go to jail, because how's he going to pay us back?" At this point, Sielski says, all they want is to recover their funds and expose Jim Gilchrist's mismanagement of the Minuteman Project.

The Fall of the Minuteman Movement

Today [September 2008] the minuteman movement is beyond mere disarray; it is in the early stages of complete decay. The arc of the Minutemen's decline and fall happens to trace almost precisely that of previous right-wing populist movements, notably the Klan of the 1920s and the militias of the 1990s. The pattern goes like this: The group is beset by financial manipulators who seem naturally drawn to them. Then, following an initial wave of popularity, the group splinters under the pressure of competing egos into smaller, more virulent entities who then unleash acts of public ugliness and violence that eventually relegate them to the fringes.

Several incidents of violence have been associated with various subfactions of the Minutemen.

The Minutemen haven't quite reached that final stage yet, but they are well on their way. And while that may be welcome news to those who oppose the Minutemen's nativist agenda, that last stage represents some natural and equally toxic consequences.

The broken promises and vicious infighting have meant, unsurprisingly, that the Minutemen's original mission—watching the border—has receded to the background. In 2007, the MCDC claimed some 2,000 volunteers at various border watches, though the on-scene reports indicated far fewer participants. In 2008, the activity dropped further, so that the annual April border watch attracted only a few dozen participants and no media coverage.

The Minuteman movement has fallen on such hard times that even Gilchrist has publicly admitted that he regrets the "Saddam Hussein mentality" within its ranks, particularly some of its smaller, independent offshoots. "Am I happy at the outcome of this whole movement? I am very, very sad, very disappointed," Gilchrist told the *Orange County [California] Register* in June [2008]. His concern may have been disingenuous, but it was far from groundless. Over the past year, several incidents of violence have been associated with various subfactions of the Minutemen. Last summer, a couple of Minutemen created a video portraying the shooting of border-crossers—which they later admitted was a hoax but decidedly a reflection of their real attitudes. The men were in a group that had spun off from the San Diego Minutemen, itself an independent offshoot of the movement.

Considering that the Minutemen were largely built on the sort of nativist appeals long favored by racist organizations, it's no surprise that racist and white-supremacist elements have been entwined with the movement since its inception. Gilchrist and Simcox both made loud noises about weeding out racist members, though in reality their "background checks" were mostly shams and covert white supremacists were silently tolerated. But even the stigma against overt racism appears to be disappearing among their organizations' successors. One border-watch group, headed by a former Minuteman Project official named Laine Lawless, went so far as to indulge in an e-mail exchange with a neo-Nazi organization offering tips on how to harass Latinos the old-fashioned way: steal from them, beat them up, mistreat their children, make death threats. This behavior has started to infect the main Minutemen organizations themselves. The MMP's official Las Vegas chapter, Americans4America, recently co-hosted an anti-immigration strategy session with officials from the white-supremacist Council of Conservative Citizens.

The Fence Remains Unbuilt

Jim Campbell was finally reimbursed in September 2007 for his $63,000 outlay for the pipe, but he wants his $100,000 back, too. His lawsuit was dismissed, and now he wants criminal action brought against Simcox and the MCDC operation. Meanwhile, nothing like Simcox's promised "high-tech, double-layered gauntlet of deterrent" has even come close to being built. "We're still hoping to finish that, basically, standing as a monument," Simcox says but adds that it's not necessary anymore and that fundraising for the project has come to a halt. (Even though the MCDC's Web site still asks visitors to "Donate to Build the Minuteman Border Fence.")

Simcox says the Minutemen declared victory when [former President George W.] Bush signed the Secure Fence Act in fall 2006, which authorized the construction of over 700 miles of double-reinforced fence along the U.S.–Mexico border. "That was really the purpose—to challenge them to do that," he says. "I just don't think we're going to get any more funding, to tell you the truth, because people see that the government's doing it. Mission accomplished."

14

The Possibility of a Pandemic Should Result in Border Closure

NBC's The Today Show

"NBC's The Today Show" is a morning news and talk show aired every morning on NBC and is the third longest running American television series

The swine flu

MEREDITH VIEIRA, co-host: Good morning. Level five. The World Health Organization now says a swine flu pandemic is imminent. In Fort Worth, Texas, all public schools ordered to shut their doors for more than a week; dozens of other schools across the nation also closed. This morning Vice President Joe Biden speaks out about the outbreak in a live interview. . . .

MATT LAUER, co-host: And I'm Matt Lauer. And this morning the Fort Worth Independent School District has closed all of its 140 schools through at least May the 8th. That's a decision that impacts some 80,000 students and of course their parents as well.

VIEIRA: And during his news conference last night, President [Barack] Obama said that it is likely that more schools across the country will do the same, and he urged parents to prepare now for that possibility. Meantime, there are con-

Meredith Vieira, Matt Lauer, Tom Costello, Vice President Joe Biden and Chuck Todd, "Broadcast Transcript," *NBC's The Today Show*, April 30, 2009. Reproduced by permission.

firmed cases of the virus in five new states: Arizona, Massachusetts, Maine, Michigan and Nevada; 94 cases in all in 11 states.

LAUER: We are going to talk to the vice president, Joe Biden, in just a couple of minutes and ask him if this government is doing enough to contain the outbreak.

Watching the Developments of Swine Flu

MATT LAUER, co-host: But first let's get to NBC's Tom Costello. He's in Washington, inside the Department of Health and Human Services with more on the story. Tom, good morning to you.

TOM COSTELLO reporting: Good morning, Matt. We're at the secretary's operation center here, where they are watching the developments and have been throughout the last few days and the night. And on this massive wall display they have got a grid of every state that currently is dealing with the swine flu as represented by these grid patterns. For example, right there over these particular Midwest states, all into Kansas and into the West Coast. And over here they're watching what's happening around the world. For example, two confirmed cases in the United Kingdom, Israel has two, Spain has two. All of this as the World Health Organization urges countries around the world to activate their pandemic emergency response plans.

With the swine flu spreading quickly across the country and globe, President Obama reiterated Wednesday night his administration is moving quickly to contain the outbreak.

President BARACK OBAMA: The key now, I think, is to make sure that we are maintaining great vigilance, that everybody responds appropriately when cases do come up.

COSTELLO: In raising the global threat level to five, the World Health Organization is now warning a swine flu pandemic is imminent.

Dr. MARGARET CHAN (World Health Organization): It really is all of humanity that is under threat during a pandemic.

COSTELLO: As more flu cases show up in cities across the US, schools and school districts with confirmed cases have been closing. From South Carolina, New York, and Connecticut in the East to Ohio, Illinois, Louisiana, Minnesota, Texas and on to Arizona and California, where in Santa Clara the school district telephoned in the middle of the night.

Fourteen hundred students got the same message.

In raising the global threat level to five, the World Health Organization is now warning a swine flu pandemic is imminent.

While most patients continue to report mild flu symptoms, the director of infectious disease at the NIH [National Institutes of Health] told lawmakers there's no way of knowing where this flu outbreak is headed.

Dr. ANTHONY FAUCI (National Institutes of Health): It could take off more, it could go dormant, it could lay low over the summer and come back in the fall.

COSTELLO: But from everyone involved, this appeal: Secretary JANET NAPOLITANO (Homeland Security Secretary): The best thing parents can do right now is to make sure you have a contingency plan in place so that you've made arrangements to care for your child in the event of a school closure.

Pres. OBAMA: If you are sick, stay home. If your child is sick, keep them out of school.

COSTELLO: Across the country state health departments report that their hotlines have been flooded and pharmacies are now reporting a run on Tamiflu and Relenza, the two anti-viral drugs that have proven to be effective in treating the symptoms. . . .

Vice President Joe Biden Discusses the Swine Flu

MATT LAUER, co-host: Joe Biden is the vice president of the United States.

Mr. Vice President, good morning. Good to see you.

Vice President JOE BIDEN: Good morning, Matt. How are you?

LAUER: I'm fine, thank you. So the World Health Organization says we're now at a level five in terms of the threat. By their definition, that means that a pandemic or epidemic over a wide geographic area is now imminent. Last night the president said no plans to shut down the borders between the US and Mexico, no plans even to curtail commercial air traffic or travel between the two countries. And I think some people this morning, Mr. Vice President, may be shaking their heads, not understanding that. Help me out.

Vice Pres. BIDEN: Well, I'll help you out by telling you that we have contacted and been in constant contact with the leading health experts both in the world as well as here in the United States, and they have suggested that that is not the way we should move. They suggested that what we should be doing is deal with mitigation, and that is the circumstances where large crowds of people, whether they're in school rooms or in soccer stadiums or in malls or whatever, where the flu is transmitted. Closing the classroom and closing the border are two fundamentally different things. And so we've been operating on the best evidence we've been given by the world's leading experts on pandemics and epidemics, and that's the advice we've been given.

LAUER: Let's just talk as nonexperts then, you and me, though. I mean, it seems the president used the analogy last night to the horse and the barn. You know, you don't close the barn door after the horse has left. But when the horse leaves the barn there aren't thousands and thousands of other horses waiting to stream out of the barn door. This is more like a water main break. It floods basements, you close down those houses and you clean them up, but you—wouldn't you also go back and turn off the water in that water main so it doesn't continue to flood other neighborhoods?

Vice Pres. BIDEN: Well, if the analogy were appropriate, yes, but I don't think the analogy is appropriate. The fact of the matter is that people who are crossing the border—the point being made by the World Health Organization is this is in other countries now. Which borders do we close? Do we close the Canadian border, too, to Canada? Do we close flights coming out of countries in Europe where it has been identified now? We're told that is not an efficacious use of our effort.

That we should be focusing on mitigation.

LAUER: Let me—let me ask this, and this is by no means a gotcha type of question, I promise. But if a member of your family came to you—no, Mr. Vice President, if a member of your family came to you and said, 'Look, I want to go on a commercial airliner to Mexico and back,' within the next week, would you think it's a good idea?

Vice Pres. BIDEN: I would tell members of my family, and I have, I wouldn't go anywhere in confined places now. It's not that it's going to Mexico, it's you're in a confined aircraft; when one person sneezes it goes all the way through the aircraft. That's me. I would not be, at this point, if I—if they had another way of transportation, suggesting they ride the subway. So from my perspective what it relates to is mitigation. If you're out in the middle of a field and someone sneezes, that's one thing; if you're in a closed aircraft or closed container . . .

LAUER: Right.

Vice Pres. BIDEN: . . . or closed car or closed classroom, it's a different thing. . . .

Mixed Messages over Swine Flu and Travel

MEREDITH VIEIRA, co-host: Let's bring in Chuck Todd. He's NBC's chief White House correspondent and political director. Good morning to you, Chuck.

> *They've been walking this line about this idea of not traveling to Mexico. They won't directly say it—and obviously we have a lot of trade with that country, it's a huge border, so instead they go around it.*

CHUCK TODD reporting: Good morning, Meredith.

VIEIRA: I can see some people watching this interview that just happened between Matt—or Sam—and Joe Biden . . .

TODD: Yeah.

VIEIRA: . . . and picking up on that and saying, 'Wait a minute, did the vice president just tell the American public don't use public transportation?'

TODD: It sure sounded like that to me. And actually, don't get on an airplane. And I think this has been the difficulty for the administration. On one hand they want to show that they have a handle on this and that they want to deal with this in a sort of community by community way, shut down schools. On the other hand, they're afraid to publicly say, 'Hey, don't go to Mexico. We're going to shut the border.' And so they've been walking this line about this idea of not traveling to Mexico. They won't directly say it—and obviously we have a lot of trade with that country, it's a huge border, so instead they go around it. 'Well, I wouldn't get on any airplane,' he said. 'I don't know if I'd go on any public transportation.' So it's a—it's a tough line, and I think that that's—it's all about not—frankly, not upsetting folks in Mexico too much.

VIEIRA: But it's a real mixed message.

TODD: It absolutely is. And at some point, you know, you have some folks on the Hill, John McCain, pretty close to advocating, 'Hey, how come we're not thinking about shutting the border?' And you do have to wonder, are they planning on it? Are they planning on a flat-out airplane ban? I mean, the first death in the United States was from somebody who flew from Mexico to the United States.

VIEIRA: You know, Chuck, last night was the president's third prime-time news conference in as many months. What was he hoping to accomplish last night?

TODD: Well, it did seem as last night he wanted to give himself a report card, try to update the American people. And you know, the White House loves these forums. They believe that it's in these events that has allowed him to build up this likability political capital. We saw it in our own NBC/Wall Street Journal poll; 81 percent tell us they like him, even 30 percent of the folks that don't agree with him on his policies. So they think this direct contact as much as possible. And I tell you, we see him all the time. He does as many of these—already three prime-time press conferences, multiple speeches, multiple town halls. It's all about making him the face not just of the White House, but he's now the face of all of government. . . .

15

The Possibility of a Pandemic Should Not Result in Border Closure

Jena Baker McNeill and James Jay Carafano

Jena Baker McNeill is a policy analyst for homeland security in the Douglas and Sarah Allison Center for Foreign Policy Studies at the Heritage Foundation, a conservative public policy institute. James Jay Carafano is the assistant director of the Heritage Foundation's Davis Institute for International Studies and a senior research fellow for national security and homeland security at the Heritage Foundation.

The swine flu [H1N1 virus] is a public health threat and needs to be dealt with through greater dissemination of information and a growth in public awareness. Though the flu has traversed the U.S.–Mexico border, closing off the border is an inappropriate response to the pandemic. Such action would not stymie transmission of the disease, but it would damage international trade. Focusing efforts on the border is wrongheaded; instead the nation should devote its resources to educating the citizenry and treating the disease in those who are infected.

The Centers for Disease Control (CDC) is reporting that, as of April 28 [2009], there have been 40 cases of swine flu in the United States. The spread of this flu and the associated deaths in Mexico have left Americans frightened and concerned. While these concerns have led to calls to contain

Jena Baker McNeill and James Jay Carafano, "Strategy for Swine Flu Should Focus on Common Sense, Not the Border," *Heritage Foundation Web Memo #2415*, April 28, 2009. Reproduced by permission.

the outbreak by closing the border with Mexico or instituting travel restrictions, a border-centric strategy is not an effective solution for dealing with the swine flu.

Instead, local health departments should focus on educating Americans about common-sense precautions individuals can take to lessen the likelihood they will be infected. Both Congress and the Department of Homeland Security (DHS) should reinforce these prudent measures rather than exacerbating fears and advocating less effective measures.

Swine Flu Outbreak

The swine flu is a viral respiratory infection that causes such symptoms as cough, body aches, fever, and joint pain. In March 2009, an outbreak of swine flu was first detected in Mexico. A month later, new cases appeared in Texas and California, followed by a larger outbreak in Mexico, which has resulted in at least 149 deaths.

As of April 28, the flu had spread to multiple countries including Canada, Spain, and New Zealand. Thus far, 40 Americans have been confirmed to be infected with the swine flu, but all are recovering and there have been no fatalities. While the flu is suspected to have begun in Mexico, the origins of the flu have not been conclusively determined.

The cases appearing in the United States have caused considerable concern among U.S. citizens and government leaders, especially given the high number of deaths of individuals infected with the virus in Mexico. In response, the World Health Organization (WHO) has designated the outbreak as a Level 4—meaning that there is "sustained human-to-human transmission" of the swine flu. DHS Secretary Janet Napolitano also issued a public health emergency declaration (a standard procedure in these situations) to ensure that resources could be given to health officials. The CDC released one-fourth of the Strategic National Stockpile of anti-viral medication as a precautionary measure.

While these are the appropriate actions to take given the number of deadly infections in Mexico and the increasing cases worldwide, more aggressive actions have also been suggested. In fact, several Members of Congress have called for the U.S. to close its border with Mexico, and many have suggested that travel restrictions are appropriate.

If someone crossing the border is infected, they could appear "asymptomatic" at the border or with symptoms virtually indistinguishable from other flus and colds.

Closing the Border Is Not the Answer

A border solution is wrong. First, doing so will not prevent infected individuals from entering the United States. If someone crossing the border is infected, they could appear "asymptomatic" at the border or with symptoms virtually indistinguishable from other flus and colds. Even the WHO has advised against the use of travel restrictions for dealing with the swine flu, emphasizing that such a measure would be ineffective.

Second, such measures would cause massive economic disruption. A blockade at the U.S.–Mexican border would effectively halt the North American supply chain. The southern border has 39 ports of entry, through which hundreds of millions of people, trucks, and cars pass each year. Mexico is America's third largest trading partner, with most goods flowing through the southern border. Given the current economic climate and the market's already skittish reaction to the swine flu, closing the border would be a crippling blow to commerce.

Finally, the flu has already gone "global"—hopes of restricting the international spread of the disease are unrealistic.

Three-Pronged Approach to Good Public Health Policy

What the United States should be doing is focusing on good public health policies. Such policies include a three-pronged approach of:

1. Treating those affected with the virus,
2. Continuing to collect useable and timely information about the flu, and
3. Educating Americans on the proper means of preventing transmission.

The origins of the flu strain have not been conclusively determined. Also, doctors are puzzled as to why the Mexican manifestations of the flu have been so deadly. Figuring out these puzzles will help to control the problem further. In the meantime, local health departments should communicate common-sense strategies to Americans, such as washing hands frequently; keeping hands out of eyes, nose, and ears; and, at the onset of flu-like symptoms, not going to work but instead going to the doctor.

Focusing on the border . . . will not stop the spread of the flu—but it will stop the economy.

These steps will go a long way toward stopping the transmission of the virus. Congress and the White House should use their leadership roles to encourage Americans to take these precautions, and they should continue to monitor the situation closely.

The United States should remain diligent in its efforts to control the spread of swine flu. This will require a common-sense approach, one reliant on the participation of all Americans to ensure that more individuals do not get sick. Focusing on the border, however, will not stop the spread of the flu—but it will stop the economy.

Organizations to Contact

The editors have compiled the following list of organizations concerned with the issues debated in this book. The descriptions are derived from materials provided by the organizations. All have publications or information available for interested readers. The list was compiled on the date of publication of the present volume; the information provided here may change. Be aware that many organizations take several weeks or longer to respond to inquiries, so allow as much time as possible.

American Enterprise Institute (AEI)
1150 17th St. NW, Washington, DC 20036
(202) 862-5800 • fax: (202) 862-7177
Web site: www.aei.org

AEI is a nonpartisan, conservative public policy organization striving to promote the ideals of free enterprise, individual opportunity, and a strong national defense. Through the sponsoring of conferences, publication of newsletters and books, and fostering of open debate, the institute seeks to achieve these goals. Institute scholars champion immigration reform that secures the U.S. borders but question the viability of building a physical barrier on the U.S.–Mexico border. Reports and commentary detailing these views are available on the AEI Web site along with a link to the bimonthly journal of the institute, the *American*.

American Immigration Control Foundation (AIC Foundation)
222 W Main St., PO Box 525, Monterey, VA 24465
(540) 468-2022 • fax: (540) 468-2024
e-mail: aicfndn@htcnet.org
Web site: www.aicfoundation.com

Beginning with its founding in 1983, the AIC Foundation has sought to reduce levels of immigration into the United States by informing the public about the negative impact of high immigration levels through its publication of books, pamphlets, booklets, and videos. Of highest concern to the organization is illegal immigration across the Mexican border into the United States, which is seen as a threat to American rule of law and a burden on U.S. society and economy. AIC Foundation publications can be purchased through the foundation's Web site.

Americas Policy Program

Center for International Policy, 1717 Massachusetts Ave. NW
Washington, DC 20016
(202) 536-2649
e-mail: americas@ciponline.org
Web site: http://americas.irc-online.org

The Americas Policy Program began 30 years ago as a project of the International Relations Center with the goal of creating a global policy agenda for the United States that emphasized the country's role as a global leader and partner. The main issues addressed by the organization are trade and economic integration, biodiversity and sustainable development, immigration, communication rights, and United States–Latin America relations. The TransBorder Project and the Border Lines Blog provide current information about U.S. border policy and actions. More information can be found on the Americas Program Web site.

Cato Institute

1000 Massachusetts Ave. NW, Washington, DC 20001-5403
(202) 842-0200 • fax: (202) 842-3490
Web site: www.cato.org

A libertarian think tank, the Cato Institute works to advance ideals such as limited government, free markets, individual liberty, and peace. With regard to immigration and labor laws, the institute advocates that an open labor market with limited restrictions on wage and hiring practices best fosters economic growth and stability. Further, the institute contends that immigration reform, not closing U.S. borders, is the key to securing the country and improving the economy. Publications of the institute include the triannual *Cato Journal*, the quarterly *Cato's Letter*, and the bimonthly *Cato Policy Report*.

Center for Immigration Studies (CIS)
1522 K St. NW, Suite 820, Washington, DC 20005-1202
(202) 466-8185 • fax: (202) 466-8076
e-mail: center@cis.org
Web site: www.cis.org

CIS is an independent, nonpartisan think tank dedicated to exploring the impact of immigration on the U.S. economy, society, and demography. The center places the national interest at the center of its discussion of immigration policy and impact, and it maintains a vision that is both pro-immigrant and low-immigration. CIS promotes border security and immigration reform that employ the latest technology while still focusing on the importance of placing agents on the border to monitor admittance. Copies of CIS backgrounders and reports, testimony, and opinion editorials as well as other multimedia materials can be accessed from the organization's Web site.

Council on Foreign Relations (CFR)
The Harold Pratt House, 58 E 68th St., New York, NY 10065
(212) 434-9400 • fax: (212) 434-9800
Web site: www.cfr.org

CFR, a nonpartisan membership organization provides unbiased information on current public policy issues in the United States. While the council does not take an official position on any issue, it does provide scholars the opportunity to voice their opinions and openly debate the topics. The CFR Web site serves as a clearinghouse of all the materials published by the organization, offering visitors the opportunity to become better informed. CFR has published backgrounders and fact sheets about U.S. border troubles and offers an analysis of different solutions in its reports and commentaries. Additional information can be found in the official publication of the council, the bimonthly *Foreign Affairs*.

Economic Policy Institute (EPI)

1333 H St. NW, Suite 300, East Tower
Washington, DC 20005-4707
(202) 775-8810 • fax: (202) 775-0819
e-mail: epi@epi.org
Web site: www.epi.org

EPI was founded in 1986 to provide a progressive voice for low- and middle-income workers in the national discussion about economic policy. Institute scholars examine the many and varied factors that impact U.S. workers with the ultimate goal of promoting a stable and thriving U.S. economy. EPI believes U.S. borders should remain open to the immigrants who help to strengthen the U.S. economy, but that immigration reform is the key to ensuring economic stability and mitigating the negative impact of illegal immigrants. The official publication of the institute is the *EPI Journal*.

Federation for American Immigration Reform (FAIR)

25 Massachusetts Ave. NW, Suite 330, Washington, DC 20001
(202) 387-3447
Web site: www.fairus.org

FAIR believes immigration reform is necessary for a sustainable U.S. economy and to maintain U.S. security. FAIR emphasizes improved border security, halting illegal immigration, and limiting immigration levels as key measures to be implemented in this reform. FAIR's work covers both legal and illegal immigration, national security, societal issues, and population growth. Detailed reports and fact sheets can be read on the organization's Web site.

Future of Freedom Foundation (FFF)

11350 Random Hills Rd., Suite 800, Fairfax, VA 22030
(703) 352-6101 • fax: (703) 352-8678
e-mail: fff@fff.org
Web site: www.fff.org

FFF believes freedom must be advanced through individual liberty, free markets, private property, and limited government. The foundation finds that currently the government takes too paternalistic a role in individuals' lives. It recognizes immigration as a crisis in the United States and believes that open borders are the only solution to the problem, worrying that current government intervention into border control could lead to socialism and eventually a police state. Commentaries about border issues and other related topics can be read on the FFF Web site.

Heritage Foundation

214 Massachusetts Ave. NE, Washington, DC 20002-4999
(202) 546-4400 • fax: (202) 546-8328
e-mail: info@heritage.org
Web site: www.heritage.org

The conservative libertarian Heritage Foundation advocates for government policies that encourage free enterprise, competition, and individual responsibility while limiting government and providing a strong national defense. The foundation believes open borders are necessary to a successful U.S. economy as they allow the free flow of goods between countries and welcome individuals who have the desire to become contributing members of U.S. society. However, the organization does believe the government has the responsibility to maintain secure borders and prevent outside threats from entering the country by increasing border patrol. Heritage WebMemos and Backgrounders, available on the foundation's Web site, provide detailed explanations of these views.

Social Science Research Council (SSRC)

One Pierrepont Plaza, 15th Fl., Brooklyn, NY 11201
(212) 377-2700 • fax: (212) 377-2727
e-mail: info@ssrc.org
Web site: www.ssrc.org

SSRC was founded in 1923 as an independent, nonprofit research organization focusing on social science at a global level. Work at the council is focused in four program areas: global security and cooperation, knowledge institutions, migration, and renewing the public sphere. One project of the SSRC focusing on U.S. border issues is the Web site *Border Battles: The U.S. Immigration Debates*. This Web site, http://borderbattles.ssrc.org, provides essays by social scientists discussing the key issues relating to immigration and U.S. border security.

U.S. Department of Homeland Security (DHS)
Washington, DC 20528
(202) 282-8000
Web site: www.dhs.gov

The DHS is the government office charged with securing the country through prevention and preparedness. It is also in charge of immigration services. In addition, the department oversees U.S. Customs and Border Protection (CBP), which is the DHS agency that physically secures the U.S. borders. The CBP's officers patrol and man the U.S. borders. Information about current DHS border programs such as the Secure Border Initiative as well as details about the CBP can be accessed from the DHS Web site.

Bibliography

Books

Edward H. Alden *The Closing of the American Border: Terrorism, Immigration, and Security Since 9/11*. New York: Harper Perennial, 2008.

Peter Andreas *Border Games: Policing the U.S.–Mexico Divide*. Ithaca, NY: Cornell University Press, 2009.

Ted Conover *Coyotes: A Journey Across Borders with America's Illegal Migrants*. New York: Vintage Books, 1987.

David J. Danelo *The Border: Exploring the U.S.–Mexican Divide*. Mechanicsburg, PA: Stackpole Books, 2008.

Miriam Davidson *Lives on the Line: Dispatches from the U.S.-Mexico Border*. Tucson, AZ: University of Arizona Press, 2000.

Jon E. Dougherty *Illegals: The Imminent Threat Posed by Our Unsecured U.S.–Mexico Border*. Nashville, TN: WND Books, 2004.

Ken Ellingwood *Hard Line: Life and Death on the U.S.–Mexico Border*. New York: Pantheon Books, 2004.

Stephen Flynn — *America the Vulnerable: How Our Government Is Failing to Protect Us from Terrorism*. New York: HarperCollins, 2004.

Tim Gaynor — *Midnight on the Line: The Secret Life of the U.S.–Mexico Border*. New York: Thomas Dunne Books, 2009.

Mark Krikorian — *The New Case Against Immigration: Both Legal and Illegal*. New York: Sentinel, 2008.

Leon C. Metz — *Border: The U.S.–Mexico Line*. Fort Worth: Texas Christian University Press, 2008.

Joseph Nevins — *Operation Gatekeeper: The Rise of the 'Illegal Alien' and the Remaking of the U.S.–Mexico Boundary*. New York: Routledge, 2002.

Tony Payan — *The Three U.S.–Mexico Border Wars: Drugs, Immigration, and Homeland Security*. Westport, CT: Praeger Security International, 2006.

Fernando Romero — *Hyperborder: The Contemporary U.S.–Mexico Border and Its Future*. New York: Princeton Architectural Press, 2008.

Periodicals

Randal C. Archibold — "Second Thoughts on Pulling the Guard from the Border," *New York Times*, June 12, 2008.

W. Ralph Basham	"A Moral Test of Our Times," *Vital Speeches of the Day*, February 2009.
Bay Buchanan	"Mexican Meltdown Threatens America," *Human Events*, February 9, 2009.
Lisa Caruso	"Border War Ahead," *National Journal Magazine*, April 11, 2009.
Eve Conant and Arian Campo-Flores	"The Enemy Within," *Newsweek*, March 23, 2009.
Monica Davey	"Drone to Patrol Part of Border with Canada," *New York Times*, December 7, 2008.
Jacques Delacroix and Sergey Nikiforov	"If Mexicans and Americans Could Cross the Border Freely," *Independent Review*, Summer 2009.
Economist	"The Border Closes," December 18, 2008.
John Geddes	"Blame Canada," *Maclean's*, December 1, 2008.
Daniel Gross et al.	"The New Dream Isn't American," *Newsweek*, May 26, 2008.
Mimi Hall	"ID Scan Gives Border Agents Leg Up," *USA Today*, November 24, 2008.
Lance Hosey	"Tear Down This Wall," *Architect*, January 2009.
Reed Karaim	"America's Border Fence," *CQ Researcher*, September 19, 2008.

Stew Magnuson	"Border Calculus," *National Defense*, July 2008.
Michelle Malkin	"The Incredible Disappearing Border Fence," *Human Events*, December 19, 2007.
John F. McManus	"The Battle Against Illegal Immigration," *New American*, March 3, 2008.
New York Times	"False Victory at the Border," July 5, 2008.
Tim Padgett	"On the Bloody Border: Mexico's Drug Wars," *Time*, April 23, 2009.
Luiza Savage	"Borderline Breakdown," *Maclean's*, May 25, 2009.
Stephanie Simon and Laura Meckler	"Border Fence Project Hits a Snag," *Wall Street Journal*, February 4, 2009.
Cam Simpson	"'Virtual Fence' Is Planned to Assess Canada Border," *Wall Street Journal*, April 1, 2009.
Geri Smith and Keith Epstein	"On the Border: The 'Virtual Fence' Isn't Working," *BusinessWeek*, February 7, 2008.
David Von Drehle	"A New Line in the Sand," *Time*, June 30, 2008.

Index

J

K

L

M

N

O

P

R

S

T